You Speak Treason

Also by Jake Highton

You Speak Treason

Jake Highton

*Emeritus journalism professor
at the University of Nevada, Reno.*

world vision
publishing

Reno, Nevada

Sketch by Jennifer Klein of the Sparks Tribune.

World Vision Publishing
© 2014 by World Vision Publishing. All rights reserved
Printed in United States of America
10 09 08 07 06   15 14 13 12 11 10 9

Library of Congress Catalog Card Number: 2013955402
Highton, Jake
A Collection of Newspaper Columns

ISBN (10) 0972717358
ISBN (13) 978-0-9727173-5-9

Why, you speak treason.

Maid Marian in
"Robin Hood."

Author's Dedication

To Andy Barbano, esteemed community leader, labor organizer, fellow Sparks Tribune columnist and friend.

Contents

Politics and Policies

Terrible legacy of Iraq war

Everyone knows that the United States is the mightiest nation in the world. Few Americans realize it is also the cruelest.

Begin with American economic sanctions imposed on Iraq 13 years before the war, depriving families of vital medicines. Then it invaded with "shock and awe," killing and destroying. After 10 years of war it decamped, leaving a frightful legacy of death, destruction and despair.

America is left with the shame and stain of one of the least justifiable wars in history. It was illegal, unconstitutional and genocidal.

Saddam Hussein was a brutal dictator but he controlled the sectarian tensions and hatred in Iraq. His ouster and the departure of Americans left the country at loggerheads: Shiites vs. Sunnis, Arabs vs. Kurds, Islamists vs. al-Qaida.

The tattered country has been left with deadly suicide bombings, blown-up buildings and car bombings.

The sanctions deprived children of medicines, condemning them to die an agonizing death. They writhed in pain in a Baghdad hospital without pain relievers. As a British nurse recalled: "The kids were wasted by water-borne diseases, the fluids ran out of their bodies and left them appearing like withered, spoiled fruit."

More cruelness. Protracted failure to restore Iraq's basic services of water, sanitation and electricity. Iraqi prisoners in Abu Ghraib led around on leashes as if they were dogs. Contamination from depleted uranium munitions and other military pollution is causing a sharp increase in congenital birth defects and cancer.

And still more. Miscarriages and premature births have risen in Iraq, especially around Fallujah. Sterility and infertility have increased.

The war toll itself is horrendous: 4,500 American killed

and 30,000 wounded. About 100,000 Iraqis civilians were killed and hundreds of thousands were displaced. Cost to U.S. taxpayers $2.2 trillion, rising to about $4 trillion in interest on borrowed money.

The wanton imperialistic invasion and intervention was all for naught. It just made the Arab World rightly abhor America.

President G.W. Bush and his evil Vice President Cheney are war criminals. Yet Cheney and other architects of the war are constantly allowed on TV to defend their crimes.

The U.N. charter, ratified by the United States, makes it clear: the U.N. Security Council must authorize war. The council refused to do so because it approves wars only for self-defense.

Self-defense was non-existent in Iraq. Instead, Bush, Cheney and Secretary of State Colin Powell presented enormous lies, including one claiming Iraq had weapons of mass destruction. Rep. John Conyers of Michigan issued a report in 2006 that showed "members of the Bush administration misstated and overstated links between Iraq and al-Qaida."

Nearly very administration for the past six decades has misled the country with deceptions and lies about wars. The military, industrial and congressional complexes fuel war fervor. And wars are immensely profitable for defense contractors, weapons makers, oil companies and suppliers of war material.

The craven corporate press, important in swaying people, also urged the war. The Washington Post and New York Times led the cheerleading, the Post in editorials and the Times with bad reporting of faulty intelligence.

Moreover, you cannot blame warmonger Bush and his fellow Republicans alone. Democrats in Congress overwhelming passed a resolution authorizing use of military force. The Constitution specifies that Congress declares war. But nowadays presidents alone declare wars, the antithesis of democracy.

Marjorie Cohn of the online Reader Supported News notes that Cheney's secret energy task force included a map of Iraqi oilfields, pipelines and refineries. It also contained "charts detailing the location of Iraqi oil and gas fields."

The date of the document: six months before 9/11. Readers will obviously conclude that the war was all about oil.

Without a draft, "supporting the troops" is easy. Relatively few Americans suffer the consequences of war. Most of those who do--the poor, the blacks and Latinos--see the military as a way to gain occupational skills while getting free food and housing and earning decent pay.

In its drive for global hegemony, the United States has much to feel guilty about, from deadly agent orange in Vietnam, senseless and secret bombing in Cambodia and all the unnecessary wars in between.

Most Americans agree the war in Afghanistan is as futile as it is brutal. But few know of the U.S. "war" in Syria: supplying arms to the rebels.

Then we have President Obama's wars in Libya and Yemen and his drone war in Pakistan. Now Obama is threatening to attack Iran, which would be an even worse disaster than Iraq.

Presidents never learn, constantly repeating the follies of the past.

Sparks Tribune, March 27, 2013

Peace Nobelist wages war

The Nobel Peace Prize committee, "betting on the come" in gambling parlance, awarded President Obama the prize in 2009 in the hope that he would bring peace.

The committee was wrong. Obama turned out to be just another perpetual war-making American politician.

He is, as his first term showed, a masterful rhetorician. But his fine words are seldom matched by deeds.

After escalating the Afghanistan War, he now promises to withdraw troops in 2014. Not likely. As Defense Secretary Leon Panetta points out: the United States is committed "to an enduring presence."

That's, what, 10, 20, 30 more years? After 11 years of wasted lives and trillions of dollars, America still has not learned that it cannot win a guerrilla war.

Yet in his second inaugural address, Obama crowed: "Whatever mistakes we have made, the plain fact is that America has helped underwrite global security for more than six decades with the blood of our citizens."

Obama is as self-deluded as far less intelligent people who talk about American exceptionalism.

Obama is fighting undeclared drone wars in Pakistan, Yemen, Somalia and Libya. He plans to establish a drone base in North Africa. Drone warfare is immoral, unethical, unconstitutional and contrary to international law.

His special operations command is carrying out "kill lists," assassinations in more than 70 countries in the purported war on terror. Budget? Secret. But that paramilitary budget is in the billions.

Collateral damage, as it is euphemistically called, is huge with 3,000 innocent men, women and children killed. Now Obama claims presidential power to launch cyberspace warfare.

America has outsourced torture to 54 nations. Columnist Robert Scheer says the rendition network has operated with "those countries most sadistic in their use of 'enhanced interrogation techniques.' "

U.S. sanctions against Iran are inhumane, leading to shortages of life-saving medicines such as chemotherapy drugs for cancer and blood-clotting devices for hemophilia.

America rattles the sabre about Iranian nuclear development but says nothing about Israeli nuclear weapons. A humane, peace-minded American president would have the political wisdom and courage to visit Iran as President Nixon went to "darkest" China decades ago.

David Swanson, online news analyst, puts it: "A hopeless spiral of delusional counter-productive approaches toward Iran needs to be broken by a 180-degree turn." True. But that would take more audacity and bravery than Obama has.

Obama vowed to close the U.S. gulag at Guantánamo, a $400,000-a-day camp that imprisons people but never charges them. It is still open, safely ensconced on Cuban soil.

Obama's second-term cabinet contains few women, blacks or Latinos but has plenty of white men and representatives of Washington's revolving-door culture.

John Brennan, Dr. Drone, named to head the CIA. Jack Lew, Wall Streeter with $2 million in salary and bonuses in 2008, named to replace Treasury Secretary Timothy Geithner, champion of Wall Street deregulation and greed. Mary Jo White named to head the Securities and Exchange Commission. She was a Morgan Stanley attorney who played a key role in squelching an SEC investigation of insider trading.

Obama is Bush II redux. He signed a five-year extension of the Foreign Intelligence Surveillance Act, including wiretapping. As David Shipler reports in The Nation:

"Obama rejects the bright sunlight of public knowledge, which is democracy's great disinfectant and cure."

Obama once campaigned as a friend of whistleblowers yet his Justice Department has launched twice as many Espionage Act prosecutions against domestic leakers as all previous administrations combined.

Chief target: Pfc. Bradley Manning. Manning did a tremendous favor to the American people by giving them important WikiLeaks information about government secrecy. Instead of being hailed as a hero, Manning is on trial for "aiding the enemy."

Obama is promoting two positive measures for his second term: a variation of his Dream Act, a path to citizenship for 11 million illegal immigrants, and stricter gun controls such as a ban on assault weapons and enormous magazines, more thorough background checks and closer monitoring of gun sales.

But Congress is talking too much about defending the borders rather than stressing the dream. As for gun controls, they are not likely to pass a gun-worshipping Congress.

David Sirota in the online column rightly concludes: "Whether railing about financial crime and then refusing to prosecute Wall Street executives or berating insurance companies and then passing a health care bill favorable to those same companies, Obama focuses more on rhetoric than on reality."

His State of the Union speech Tuesday was more of the same: glowing words but just words.

Ames Tribune (Iowa), Feb. 21, 2013

2 Obama policies deplored

Quarrels with President Obama are many but none greater than his outrageous policies on whistleblowers and drones.

His administration's treatment of whistleblower Pfc. Bradley Manning is unconscionable. For two and one-half years Manning has been held in a military prison, subject to torture and other inhumane treatment. Locked up naked in a cage, driven half mad. It's one more terrible blot on the American historic escutcheon.

Manning's crime? Supplying a trove of documents to the world, documents that are no threat to national security but a gross embarrassment to America.

The government charge of "aiding the enemy" is patently absurd. He merely wanted to provoke "worldwide discussion, debate and reform." The world rewarded him with much discussion and debate. Reform, alas, is beyond the capacity of the U.S. government.

"His repressive treatment," Ed Pilkington of the UK Guardian declared, "is one of the disgraces of Obama's first term. He not only defended Manning's treatment but also as commander in-chief of court martial judges improperly decreed his guilt when he asserted that he broke the law."

Manning is a classic whistleblower. The public appreciates his leak of astonishing examples of systematic U.S. subversion of worldwide democracy, including killings and atrocities. Governments do not appreciate such candor.

Governments abroad react the same way with another great leaker, Julian Assange. He too is considered an "enemy of the state" by the British.

Assange released hundreds of thousands of diplomatic cables showing U.S. war crimes, collusion with death squads in Iraq, machinations and lies of U.S. allies and spying on U.N. officials.

U.S. politicians and right-wingers want Assange designated as a terrorist. An absurdity. But nothing is absurd to a U.S. government determined to conceal embarrassment.

First Amendment rights of Manning and Assange are being denied. As so often in hypocritical America, free speech has its limits.

The drone policy is clearly immoral. Who can and cannot be targeted is vague. Terrorists are the supposed aim but the number of innocents killed increases.

So-called "signature strikes" allow the CIA to fire missiles even when it doesn't even know the identities of those who could be killed. The policy is shrouded in the usual CIA secrecy.

But it is known that the drones have killed thousands in Afghanistan, Pakistan, Yemen and Somalia. Such a policy is a great recruiting tool for the Taliban. It is one answer to the President G.W. Bush question: why do they hate us?

They hate America for many reasons like invading and occupying Iraq on trumped up charges.

First and foremost, the invasion once again dented the notion of American exceptionalism, the idea that America is always righteous.

The toll is grim: 4,487 American lives lost, 32,226 Americans wounded and many suffering from post-traumatic stress disorder. Cost: $1 trillion.

Iraq casualties? Upwards of 115,000.

The Iraq War should weigh forever on the Bush conscience--if Bush had a conscience.

Cynical reactionaryism

The elevation of Rep. Tim Scott of South Carolina to the Senate might move some benighted crackers to marvel about "how far we have come."

Scott will be the first black senator from South Carolina since Reconstruction. He is also fiercely anti-tax, anti-union and anti-abortion. His selection by Gov. Nikki Haley is reactionary.

Military and sex

The military's notorious culture of sexual violence is reaching record highs at the three military academies with 80 *reported* assaults over the academic year just concluded. (Many sexual assaults are not reported.)

Meanwhile, the Veteran Affairs Department shines what the New York Times calls "a troubling light" on the experience of Iraq and Afghanistan veterans. A clinical psychologist with the National Center for PTSD said that a survey of 2,348 vets of those wars showed that half the women and 10 percent of the men had been sexually assaulted.

Such evidence makes it clear that women suffer a largely hidden burden in combat zones.

Fallen idol

How are the mighty fallen.
2 Samuel, 1:25

Lance Armstrong spun a great sports yarn: how he overcame cancer to win the Tour de France--the most prestigious race in cycling--seven times.

Doubters said it was impossible to win the Tour without cheating. They were right. The U.S. Anti-Doping Agency detailed how Armstrong's Postal Service team doped its way to triumph.

Testosterone, EPO and blood-doping: a gigantic fraud. Riders say they must cheat to stay competitive. Better to lose than win dishonorably. But that is now a hopelessly utopian notion.

Ames (Iowa) Tribune, Jan. 11, 2013

Snowden, Manning: 'dangerous' heroes

The most dangerous man in America.

> Government label for Daniel Ellsberg after he released Pentagon Papers revealing U.S. lies and deceptions during the Vietnam War.

America's government under President Obama has become a Surveillance State with its National Security Agency spying at home and abroad.

Before whistleblower Edward Snowden was recently granted asylum in Russia, Attorney General Eric Holder declared that Russian President Putin should turn him over to the United States because fears of torture and execution were groundless.

It's a sad reflection that America has to tell the world that it is a decent nation, not like those torturers and executioners in other countries.

Yet the shameful truth is that America refuses to close Guantánamo with its brutal treatment of prisoners and its years of detention without charges. The CIA has used "black sites" for torture overseas. America does not respect international law with its terrorist campaign of drone attacks and special operations forces abroad.

As for Obama, he was so incensed by Putin's decision that he canceled talks in Moscow. But many Americans and much of the world were thankful for Snowden's disclosures.

The NSA is the largest bureaucracy in the overstuffed U.S. security complex, what Nation magazine called "a farrago of draconian harshness and dodgy legality masked by solemn appeals to the rule of law." The New York Times pointed out "the national security apparatus has metastasized into a vast and unchecked exercise in government secrecy and the overzealous prosecution of those who breach it."

Snowden released the documents because he refused to allow "the U.S. government to destroy privacy and basic liberties." His view got scant support in the corporate media.

David Gregory of NBC's "Meet the Press" considered Snowden a criminal for leaking classified national security material. (Leaking is a crime only to the secrecy-obsessed government that classifies 92 million documents a year.) Jeffrey Toobin, New Yorker columnist, blasted Snowden as "a grandiose narcissist who deserves to be in prison."

The Times, suggesting that Manning "suffered delusions of grandeur," called him reckless. And some in the media used a classic putdown: Manning is gay. His release of documents indicated a "conflicted personality."

Washington politicians weighed in, declaring that Snowden committed the ultimate crime by revealing how broadly the government is collecting phone and Internet records of Americans. The huffing was non-partisan. Republican House Speaker John Boehner said: "He's a traitor." Democratic Senator Dianne Feinstein said: "It's an act of treason."

Meanwhile, another whistleblower, Private First Class Bradley Manning, faces a lifetime in prison.

A military court pronounced him guilty of violating the Espionage Act, a World War I law that President Nixon resurrected for his vendetta against Ellsberg. It called Manning's release of 700,000 documents one of the greatest betrayals in U.S. history. In other words, a Benedict Arnold!

Manning, who revealed the extent of spying on the American people and even worldwide diplomats, is a scapegoat for U.S. wrongs in Afghanistan and Iraq and the unconstitutional Guantánamo prison. As media observer

Noam Chomsky put it: "Manning is a hero. He is letting people know what their government is doing in secret.

A U.N. special report on torture noted that U.S. treatment of Manning was "cruel, inhuman and degrading." The San Francisco Chronicle said: "The military treatment of Manning has been shocking, the Obama administration's prosecution odious."

It was indeed. After his arrest in 2010 Manning was isolated in the Marine Corps brig in Quantico, Virginia, awakened every five minutes during the day and made to stand at attention naked at night.

Yet Obama, the nation's peerless leader and Nobel Peace Prize winner, assured Americans that such treatment was for Manning's own good. It's disgraceful when the president has such bestial values.

The Obama administration has brought twice as many Espionage Act charges than all previous administrations combined. Obama, of all people, should know better. As a civil rights attorney and constitutional law professor, he presumably read Orwell's lament about "thought police" and "big brother." But he acts as if he had never read "1984."

Manning's view is simple: he wanted to provoke "worldwide discussion, debate and reform." (The last things the government wants.)

He was morally right to expose war crimes. Under international law he had an obligation to do so. The Geneva Conventions and the Nuremberg Charter support him.

Nevertheless, he was forced to endure a show trial. Military "justice" is injustice.

Manning is a serious, earnest young man. His dog tag proclaims his cause: "humanity."

Sparks Tribune, Aug. 15, 2013

15

All hail leaker Manning

Pfc. Bradley Manning, sentenced to 35 years in prison by a military court, deserves two things: a presidential pardon and the Nobel Peace Prize.

President Obama has made plain his hostility to the heroic leaker so the odds are 5,000-to-1 against a pardon. Nor are the Peace Prize deciders in Oslo likely to honor Manning with such a prestigious award.

But you never know about them. The "wizards" gave a peace prize to Obama in 2009 for his noble rhetoric-- not his deeds. (The Obama award was an Orwellian judgment worthy of "war is peace.")

As Truthout reminds us, Manning's honesty is being punished. Presidents and Congress, dragging the nation into unnecessary wars and ordering torture and imprisonment without trial, go unpunished. U.S. politicians never are subject to "truth squads" like South Africa's Truth and Reconciliation Committee.

Manning's WikiLeaks included a video taken during an American helicopter attack in Baghdad showing the slaughter of civilians. That is hardly treasonous. He released diplomatic cables, dossiers of detainees at Guantánamo never tried and recounted U.S. crimes in Iraq and Afghanistan. That is hardly treasonous. His whistleblowing revealed drone strikes in Yemen, the American-backed coup in Honduras and U.S. use of cluster bombs. That is hardly treasonous.

The ACLU had it right: "When a soldier who shared information with the press is punished something is seriously wrong with the military justice system. A system that doesn't distinguish between leaks in the public interest and treason will not only produce unjust results but deprive the public of information necessary for accountability."

Clemenceau said it best: "Military justice is to justice what military music is to music."

Hillary beat outrageous

Here in the wilds of Nevada the daily doorstep delivery of the New York Times is essential. This columnist needs facts to back up his opinions. He gets them in the Times, the best newspaper in the world.

But the Times sometimes manifests poor editorial judgment. Such a case was the recent establishment of a Hillary Clinton beat *three years before* the presidential election.

It is not just unfair, giving Ms. Clinton a platform that other potential candidates do not have. It compels a Hillary beat reporter to be tedious long before few care about the race or the candidates. Above all, it forces the paper to manufacture news.

It is absurdity multiplied.

Besides, the Times already has columnist Maureen Dowd who tells the truth about Hillary and the Clinton clan. Her recent column was devastating. Its headline: "Money, money, money, money, MONEY."

She wrote:

• "The Clinton Foundation is more interested in raising billions for her presidential bid in 2016 than doing charitable works." (It takes billions to mount a serious presidential bid, money that no other candidate is likely to have.)

• "Bill Clinton earned $17 million last year giving speeches, including one to a Lagos company for $700,000." He demanded $500,000 to speak in Israel but the Israelis, rejecting the bid, rightly thought the fee ridiculous. Hillary gets $200,000 a speech.

In contrast, Dowd points out that former President Carter "quietly goes around the world eradicating Guinea worm disease" and another ex-president, Harry Truman, struggled on his Army pension of $112.56 a month.

Truman, a man with incredible integrity, said: "I could never lend myself to any transaction, however respectable, that would commercialize the prestige and dignity of the presidency." The Clintons have no such scruples.

George Parker of the New Yorker observed: "The top of American life has become a cozy and lucrative place where the social capital of who you are and who you know brings unimaginable returns."

Columnist Dowd concludes by skewering the clan: "The Clintons want to do big worthy things but they also want to squeeze money from rich people all over the world, insatiably gobbling up cash for politics, charity and themselves."

Scalia defines argle-bargle

Supreme Court Justice Antonin Scalia is smug, self-satisfied and usually judicially "wrong."

In a spring the court correctly invalidated the Defense of Marriage Act that said marriage is only between a man and a woman. Scalia, dissenting, attacked the 5-4 majority for "legalistic argle-bargle."

In a recent speech to a lawyer's group in San Francisco, Scalia was asked the meaning of argle-bargle. He said it meant nonsense.

Webster's Third Edition New International Dictionary, unabridged and weighing 12 and one-half pounds, defines the word as meaning argument or dispute. The dictionary adds that in Scots dialect it means a "lively discussion." (More recent usage calls for argy-bargy spelling.)

So in one sense Scalia is right. Most Supreme Court justices write opinions supporting their *political* opinions. The result is often legalistic nonsense: argle-bargle.

Sparks Tribune, Aug. 29, 2013

Heroic Manning judicially lynched

Photographs from the court-martial trial of Army Pfc. Bradley Manning in Fort Meade, Maryland, reveal much about him and his character.

• He is splendid in his dress uniform, beribboned and wearing a perky military beret. Every inch a soldier.

• He looks like the computer geek he is, bespectacled, brainy.

• Burly guards who lead him to and from the courtroom make him look puny, at five feet, two inches, too harmless to be an enemy of the people.

But the Pentagon and President Obama think otherwise. They have already convicted him of betraying the country. In so doing they have declared war on the truth.

Bradley Manning is a hero, a man of conscience who is willing to sacrifice an Army career for the greater good of America. But he won't get justice in a military court. Instead he will be judicially lynched.

During pretrial hearings the judge, Colonel Denise Lind, said her orders were secret. When the trial opened, she ruled that all evidence presented by the defense was irrelevant.

So the defense is muzzled. It is not allowed to point out that Manning had a moral and legal obligation under international law to expose U.S. war crimes. Colonel Lind even refused to allow the defense to challenge the government's false assertion of harm to national security.

In the words of the Queen of Hearts in "Alice's Adventures in Wonderland": "sentence first--verdict afterwards."

Manning admits that he released 700,000 diplomatic cables and documents. He also released a 2007 video of a U.S. helicopter pilots nonchalantly gunning down Iraqi civilians and two Reuters reporters.

"The most alarming aspect of the video was the delight in bloodlust," Manning said in his statement of conscience. "They dehumanized the individuals they were engaging by referring to them as 'dead bastards' and congratulating each other on the ability to kill in large numbers."

Matt Taibbi of Rolling Stone called the trial "an incredible act of institutional vengeance." It is that. It also reveals how U.S. leaders preach democracy but, in effect, call democracy the enemy.

Media critic Norman Solomon asks: "Who is aiding the enemy, the whistleblowers or the perpetrators?" The answer is obvious. Nevertheless, Obama rails against whistleblowers like Manning, Julian Assange and Edward Snowden.

"What Manning did for his country was priceless," Michael Ratner of the online Truthout says. Yet Manning has already paid a steep price.

He was held in solitary confinement for 23 hours a day for five months. He was forced to sleep naked for two months. His sleep was deliberately broken three times a night. As a U.N. special investigator reported: "Manning was subjected to cruel, inhuman and degrading treatment." In a word: torture.

Daniel Ellsberg, who revealed the truth about government lies in the Pentagon Papers, wrote: "A military and government dedicated to upholding justice and democracy on a global scale must not use secrecy to hide from their own crimes." But they are doing just that. And for that Manning will probably spend the rest of his life in prison.

"He made a profoundly important moral decision," Ellsberg declared. "I believe history will honor him." And vindicate him too.

Manning's 35-page conscience statement is powerful and moving. He placed his "conscience above personal safety and liberty for the public good and the moral imperative of carrying out acts of defiance."

• He "had the temerity to report to the outside world the indiscriminate slaughter, war crimes, torture and abuse carried out by U.S. occupation forces in Iraq and Afghanistan."

• "The cables and documents are embarrassing but essential."

• "It is a concerted effort by the security and surveillance state to extinguish what is left of a free press." (Although that "free press" was found wanting in the Los Angeles Times and New York Times, both papers refusing to print Manning's WikiLeaks.)

Ray McGovern of the online Consortium News calls Manning a biblical prophet, putting him in the tradition of Abraham.

"Prophets will neither acquiesce to injustice nor hide wrongdoing," McGovern writes. "Whereas biblical stories are largely myth and cannot be read as history, they often witness to truth in a way that mere history cannot."

Mark 6:4 quotes Jesus as describing the American way two centuries ago: "a prophet is not without honor but in his own country."

Obama is unworthy of the Nobel Peace Prize. Manning is.

Ames (Iowa) Tribune, June 20, 2013

Congressman wins chutzpah trophy

Rep. Stephen Fincher of Tennessee has already won the 2013 chutzpah award.

Fincher, testifying recently on the farm bill before the House Agricultural Committee, denounced the food stamp program in the bill as "stealing other people's money."

He defended extreme cuts in the monies for nutrition assistance by invoking the Bible: "The one who is unwilling to work shall not eat." (2 Thessalonians 3:10, New International version)

A few days later Fincher was still harping on that theme: "The role of citizens, of Christians, of humanity, is to take care of each other, not for Washington to steal and give to others."

Yet in one of the grossest instances of hypocrisy ever to come out of Congress, Fincher did not mention that as a Tennessee farmer he has collected a staggering $3.5 million in farm subsidies from 1999 to 2012.

According to the Agriculture Department, in 2012 Fincher received a check for $70,000, his share of the subsidy given to farmers and farmland owners even if they do not grow crops.

Boy Scout bias

The Boys Scouts of America has repealed the ban on gay scouts but it's only half a loaf: it still forbids gay and lesbian leaders.

"It ducked the chance for a principled repudiation of bigotry in favor of equivocation," the New York Times editorialized. "The message to young people is still: if you're gay, keep quiet, there is something wrong with you. Boy scouting still equates homosexuality with deviance."

The Girl Scouts have long adopted modern thinking, allowing gay scouts and gay and lesbian leaders. To protest

Boy Scout discrimination, Eagle Scouts might consider sending back their badges and explaining why.

Offensive Obama travel

The cost of flying Air Force One from Washington to President Obama's home state of Illinois is $180,000 an hour. Hardly a big budget item.

But it is offensive when federal workers are forced to take unpaid furloughs. It is offensive when federal agencies are closed. It is offensive when White House tours are canceled. It is offensive when Obama flies to Florida for golf with Tiger Woods. It is offensive when he flies to Aspen, Colo., so his daughters can ski.

Congressman Chris Stewart of Utah put it well: "The president is asking the people to sacrifice but not himself."

Wealthy advisers

Meanwhile Obama continues to pack his second-term Cabinet with wealth galore. His latest rich adviser is Michael Froman, nominated as trade representative.

Froman manages a $500,000 Citigroup fund stashed away in the Grand Cayman's Ugland House, symbol of tax avoidance.

The New York Times reports that the "modest whitewashed building" is headquarters for "19,000 business entities seeking favorable tax treatment." Froman also received millions of dollars to divest himself from Wall Street investments that rely on a tax loophole.

Money rules Washington, Congress and Obama too.

Fond farewell

One of the greatest gifts of the gods is laughter. Jean Stapleton was a great gift. As the Times put it in a headline: "The miracle of a ditz with depth."

Stapleton, who died recently, starred in "All in the Family," a marvelous TV show in which she played Edith, the wife of the bigoted Archie Bunker (Carroll O'Connor).

Archie was an irascible loading-dock worker who was white, male, conservative and wildly patriotic. He bullied Edith, infuriated his liberal son-in-law (Rob Reiner) and barely tolerated his daughter (Sally Struthers).

But Edith, a symbol of emergent feminism in the 1970s, provided the subtle, soft laughter of a compassionate, kind liberal with a serious purpose: demolish bigotry. She succeeded admirably, winning three Emmy Awards doing so while "All in the Family" topped the Nielsen ratings for five consecutive seasons.

Crush the infamy

Monarchs always live beyond a nation's means.

The Netherlands gives its king, Willem-Alexander, a tax-free annual salary of $1.1 million plus $5.7 million for personnel and expenses. His wife, Maxima, gets a tax-free salary of $425,000 and $750,000 for expenses. The king sold a holiday villa mansion in Mozambique only after public protest at such extravagance.

Meanwhile the Dutch government has slashed subsidies for art museums, theater, opera and orchestras.

No wonder Hans Maessen of the tiny Dutch New Republican Fellowship wants to abolish the monarchy. He's absolutely right to end this centuries-old absurdity. But the numbers are against him.

Hard as it to believe, the Dutch worship their royals. The Netherlands is probably the most liberal nation in the world yet it clings to a reactionary monarchy.

Of all human follies, monarchy is one of the greatest.

Sparks Tribune, June 13, 2013

Plunging down corporate rabbit hole

Whatever hope many of us had in 2008 for electing Barack Obama president is rendered ridiculous by his recent naming of Penny Pritzker as secretary of commerce.

"The despicable appointment boosts corporate power and shafts the public," social critic Norman Solomon writes. "Obama's frequent boast of standing up for working people against special interests tumbles, his integrity becomes laughable."

Pritzker was Obama's heavyweight fundraiser both as U.S. Senate candidate in Illinois and as a presidential candidate. She's worth $1.85 billion, one of the 300 wealthiest American, and heir to the Hyatt Regency hotel chain and serves on its board.

She and the Hyatt are viciously anti-union, a stance that helped swell Hyatt's fortune. Offshore tax havens and $600 million in tax credits have also bolstered the Pritzker family wealth.

Investigative journalist Dennis Bernstein reported: "Her sub-prime operation for Superior Bank in Chicago targeted poor and working people of color. She ended up crashing Superior, a billion-dollar cost to taxpayers and a tragedy for the 1,400 people who lost their savings."

In 2001 the federal government recognized the fraud, fining Pritzker and her family $460 million for "predatory, deceitful and racist tactics at Superior."

Yet none of that enormous wealth and sullied record deterred President Obama. As Norman Solomon put it, paraphrasing Alice in Wonderland, he dipped into plunderland and went down the corporate rabbit hole.

Meanwhile, our noble president chose Tom Wheeler, another Obama megafundraiser, to head the Federal Communications Commission.

Former FCC commissioner Nicholas Johnson pointed out the truth: "Wheeler's background is as a trade association representative for companies appearing before the commission, a lobbyist in Congress and a venture capitalist investing in and profiting from others whose requests he will be ruling on."

Government largesse to the wealthy never ceases. Officials leave one branch of government to serve in another. They never challenge corporate power, help enrich their pals and ignore consumers.

Zinn and unions

The late historian Howard Zinn espoused unions, not just for decent pay, but for the essentials of human dignity: a safe work environment and robust health insurance and retirement benefits.

Zinn, in "A People's History of the United States," quoted critic Richard Hofstadter: "the public saw Teddy Roosevelt as the great lover of nature and physical fitness, the war hero, the Boy Scout in the White House. But the advisers to whom TR listened were almost exclusively representatives of industrial and finance capital."

Just like Obama.

Yet so many Americans today are anti-union and therefore anti-worker. That view is unfathomable, holding business interests over rights of workers.

Do American people know that 4,500 American workers are killed each year on the job?

The recent tragedies in Bangladesh and the West Chemical and Fertilizer Co. in Texas cry out for unions to protect workers from death and injury.

The Texas attorney general brags about his euphemistically called "right to work" state. But the deaths in the Texas explosion suggest the "right to die" state is more appropriate.

The plant had stored 270 tons of ammonium nitrate, 1,350 times more than required to trigger Department of Homeland Security oversight, Nation magazine noted.

The company violated six federal and state regulations in the past decade, paid minimal fines and had not been inspected by the Occupational Safety and Health Administration for 28 years.

The capitalist way of saving money by not meeting safety codes is far more important than saving "mere" lives.

The situation for unionless workers in Bangladesh is similar. At Rana Plaza factory owners refused to evacuate the building after huge cracks appeared in the walls. The result: 1,127 lives lost, 2,500 injured.

One hundred and twelve employees burned to death or perished jumping to their deaths at another Bangladesh plant in November. In that case plant owners did not build fire escapes. But they did lock doors "to prevent theft."

Corporate response to these disasters? "Always the same: vague promises and public relations dodges while the pile of corpses grows," Scott Nova of the Workers Rights Consortium says.

Bangladesh clothing manufacturers turn out cheap products by ignoring safety regulations and paying slave wages of 21 cents an hour.

The conscience of shoppers at stores like Wal-Mart should be seared. The low prices they enjoy come at the cost of outsourcing and plantation treatment of workers.

Sparks Tribune, May 23, 2013

Romney bungled campaign

The worst one did not win.
Cuban state website

Mitt Romney ran an idiotic campaign, running for president on a reactionary platform.

He alienated women. He alienated Latinos. He alienated 47 percenters. He alienated 99 percenters.

Only obtuse politicians fail to realize that the country has become browner, blacker and more Asian.

Romney's anti-immigration policy was a failure. The country was built on immigrants and continues to need immigrants, legal or not. His war on women was a failure, as such an outrageous policy should be.

His desire to privatize Medicare was a failure, as it should have been. He wanted to gut Social Security, essential to so many retirees. He referred to 47 percenters with the equivalent of the Reaganesque sneer, "welfare queens."

You cannot win a presidential election by running to the right. This is a conservation nation but the bulk of the voters are middle-of-the-roaders. Romney's main support came from older white males, Tea Party retrogrades and fellow plutocrats.

Perhaps one good thing did come out of the Romney campaign: many Americans should now realize that Mormons are not a cult but just another form of Christianity. Mormons are good people. They deserve the tolerance of all faiths.

As for Romney himself, he is politically extinct. His party is an endangered species. It stubbornly clings to Bush tax cuts for $250,000 incomes. It bashes gays, opposes gay marriage.

Many on the GOP right-wing are anti-science, procreationist. They foolishly oppose climate change. They try to suppress votes of millions, often claiming non-existent voter fraud.

"For a party that has built itself up on an explicit and implicit appeals to xenophobia, cultural resentment and income redistribution for the rich, ideological purity is not a strategy for success," the New York Times pointed out.

The GOP-controlled House is full of cretins. It is so obstructionist it tries to thwart Obama rather than legislating for the needs of America.

The Senate is thwarted by GOP filibustering. Democratic leader Harry Reid admitted twice in recent years that he regrets leaving the filibuster in place. Twice he failed to abolish it.

President Obama was easily re-elected but progressives are hardly rejoicing.

Obama has the "slows" about the Afghanistan War, costing thousand of lives and billions of dollars. He refuses to reduce the military empire. His drone attacks on other nations, killing civilians, are illegal.

He supports the heinous Israeli policy toward the Palestinians in general and the assaults on Gaza specifically, a policy cruelly called by the Israelis as "periodic grass-cutting" of militants. Obama considers whistleblowers criminals.

He targets militants for assassination, even U.S. citizens. He refuses to close Guantánamo. He signed a bill allowing indefinite detention of terrorist suspects without trial. His feds harass harmless medical marijuana dispensaries.

But the 2012 vote did produce joy in the election of Elizabeth Warren of Massachusetts to the U.S. Senate. She created the Consumer Protection Bureau but the gutless Obama refused to appoint her as consumer advocate.

The election also produced delight by the elevation of

Rep. Tammy Baldwin of Wisconsin to the Senate. She will be the country's first openly gay senator.

Joe Donnelly of Indiana deservedly won a Senate seat because his opponent stupidly called contraception by rape "God's will." And Sen. Claire McCaskill of Missouri was happily re-elected because her opponent ignorantly said victims of "legitimate rape" would not get pregnant.

The only state that Obama won that did not elect a Democratic senator was Nevada. It chose Sen. Dean Heller over Rep. Shelley Berkeley. A shame. Berkeley is far superior to the lightweight Heller.

But an ethics problem defeated Berkeley. She was accused of pushing for a kidney-care center in Las Vegas and Medicaid reimbursements for kidney patients while her doctor husband is a kidney specialist in Las Vegas.

Politicians must be like Caesar's wife: above suspicion.

Referendum results

• Gay marriage is now legal in nine states: Connecticut, Iowa, Maine, Maryland, Massachusetts, New Hampshire, New York, Vermont and Washington. Nine states down, 41 to go.

• The heinous three-strikes-and-you're-out law has been softened by California voters. A third felony conviction, no matter how trivial, no longer draws an automatic lifetime prison sentence. The New York Times noted correctly that "three strikes" was one of the "most destructive and unfair sentencing policies in the nation."

• Colorado and Washington wisely legalized smoking marijuana for recreational use. Pot is harmless. Alcohol and tobacco are not. Two states down, 48 to go.

• Unfortunately, abolition of the death penalty was defeated in California. Capital punishment is inhumane, unworthy of America.

Sparks Tribune, Nov. 22, 2012

'Joe six pack' now peacenik

In this weak piping time of peace.
                                        Richard III

President Obama, the Great Black Hope, has become as shallow and shabby as any white politician. He is a tragic figure.

Cornel West, black intellectual and social critic, laments: "He is a shell of a man. There is no deep conviction. There is no connection to anything bigger than he is."

Historian Norman Pollack is bitter, describing Obama as "the reformer manqué, blithely dealing out death. The 'humanitarian' Obama personally oversees a worldwide terror network of drones that 'bugsplat' people, their rescuers and mourners."

All Obama's soaring rhetoric masks a man without mind, heart and courage.

It would have taken all three qualities to say no immediately to a strike against Syria. Instead, Obama agonized, photographed often with a wrinkled brow and a deadly serious mien. Oh, the terrible burden of the presidency!

New York Times columnist Maureen Dowd writes that even "Joe Six Pack is now a peacenik." William Greider, writing for The Nation, adds:

• "The American people are fed up with intervening in other people's wars. Iraq and Afghanistan taught bitter lessons."

• "Militarism and the military=industrial-congressional complex are losing their iron grip on U.S. politics."

• "The U.S. military has become the gravest threat to peace."

In 2002 an Illinois legislator decried the Iraq War, "a

31

rash war, a war based not on reason but passion, a war distracting the country from its own problems." The speechmaker? Obama.

The saber rattling, warmongering and imperialist Obama should have heeded what he said himself. He should have listened to critics opposing the sending of cruise missiles into Syria. Even planning a deadly strike destroys Obama's credibility.

The United States continues to play the world's moral cop yet its hypocrisy is gross. For a century it has intervened, invaded and bombed other nations.

Fighting in Vietnam, America used napalm. It sprayed huge amounts of Agent Orange that is still harming its people five decades later. The CIA was complicit with Saddam Hussein's use of chemical weapons in the Iraq war.

America hammered Fallujah in Iraq with depleted uranium and used white phosphorus against combatants. People in Fallujah still suffer today from cancer, birth defects and child deformities.

Gary Younge, UK Guardian columnist, writes: this sorrowful record "stands squarely at odds with its pretensions of moral authority."

Yet Obama insisted an attack was the only moral response after Syrian President al-Bashar Assad gassed his own people. In other words, tit for tat: America would kill innocent Syrian civilians to compensate for Assad's evil deed.

Although bombing Syria would be illegal under international law, Obama sounded determined to strike even if Congress disapproves. He claims presidential "authority to carry out this action without specific congressional approval."

Obama declared: "This menace must be confronted." He insisted military action would be "limited, narrow," with "no boots on the ground." But those are oft told lies.

Super hawk Secretary of State Kerry egged on the president, mounting an international full-court press demanding military intervention. But even Congress, a historic war backer, balked at giving the president authority to start another war.

However, the powerful Senate Majority Leader, Harry Reid, is a contemptible third-rater. He never learns anything important. As the Reno News & Review editorialized: "Neither in the House nor Senate did Reid ever oppose the use of force by presidents in a dozen different international disputes."

One solution might have been to turn the matter of chemical weapons over to the International Court.

Unfortunately, the United States is not one of the 122 nations backing the ICC, declaring that it interferes with America's sovereignty. It's a spurious argument. It tells the world that America doesn't believe in international law.

Striking a sovereign territory without its consent, without a sensible self-defense rationale and without approval of Congress and the U.N. Security Council is beyond the pale. An attack would just increase Arab hatred of America already at a fever pitch.

In any case, Russia may have saved Obama from a historic blunder. It proposed and the United States agreed that Syria destroy its cache of chemical weapons.

As for the two and one-half year civil war in Syria, some of the rebels led by Islamist extremists kill innocents. Video shows other rebels executing captured government soldiers.

Britain, long a U.S. poodle, has finally comes to its senses with a ringing "no." Yet in America we have a Nobel Peace Prize winner pleading for war.

Obama has forgotten everything and learned nothing from history.

Sparks Tribune, Sept. 19, 2013

Social Issues

Radical King's justice distant

Most Americans today praise Martin Luther King, one of America's great heroes. They laud his fight for racial equality. They admire his "I Have a Dream" speech. But precious few Americans know of his radicalism, his other battles for social justice and a decent America.

King, who led 250,000 people on the great March on Washington 50 years ago, opposed the Vietnam War.

"If America's soul becomes totally poisoned, part of the autopsy must read Vietnam," King said. "A nation that continues year after year to spend more money on the military than on programs of social uplift is approaching spiritual death." (Even more true today.)

He attacked the savagery of capitalism. He called for an increase in the minimum wage. He criticized the yawning gap between the rich and poor. (The gap is growing ever wider.) He urged universal health care, angered that this rich country did not have it while Britain and Scandinavian countries did.

No wonder the FBI hounded him, sending false reports to the media slandering him and calling him a communist.

As for "I Have a Dream," it may be the greatest speech ever delivered in America. Its marvelous cadences ("justice rolls down like waters"), the contrasting metaphors ("desolate valley of segregation to the sunlit path of racial justice") and resonating repetitions of "I have a dream" and "let freedom ring."

The night before he was murdered in 1968 at a motel in Memphis, Tenn., he spoke to the striking sanitation workers. "The issue is the refusal of Memphis to be fair to its public servants," he told them. "America must be true to what it says on paper about justice."

He was first, last and always for justice. Genesis 37:19, 20 records: "Behold this dreamer cometh...let us slay him." He was slain while going to Memphis to seek justice for sanitation workers.

Yet 50 years after the great assembly in Washington the nation has not reached the "promised land" that the dreamer dreamed of.

Local celebration marred

About 50 supporters of the Reno-Sparks NAACP recently crowded the sidewalk in front of the federal building in Reno to mark the 50th anniversary of the March on Washington. The group was small but celebrated with fervor. Many passing motorists honked in approval.

But the event was badly blemished by deliberate disruptions by a courthouse worker.

The guy started a noisy weed eater just as the group was gathering. Then, in the words of Andy Barbano, celebration organizer and Sparks Tribune columnist: "He went from annoying to obnoxious."

The worker threw the NAACP banner and an event sign on the ground and then stepped on them. While the participants were speaking, he deliberately fired up his loud lawnmower, drowned out the speaker, ran the dangerous machine perilously close to the assembly and knocked one woman to the ground.

When an angry Barbano ran up to him to complain, the worker flung an obscenity at him while continuing his careening.

One of the celebrants, former NAACP president Lonnie Feemster, decried the worker's "rude and reckless behavior" and denounced his intrusions as uncalled for.

Indeed it was all of that. The worker could have acted only under the orders of the federal Homeland Security officer on duty. That guard disrupted the assembly by making it move away from the steps although the building was closed and no one was entering or leaving.

Feemster should have sent his justified complaint to the guard's boss, President Obama.

Bankruptcy 2nd to sports

Detroit, once thriving with car manufacturing and sales, has filed for bankruptcy. But Motor City sports fans need not worry: the city will build a $650 million hockey arena for the Detroit Red Wings.

The owner of the Red Wings is a billionaire who could afford to pay for the arena. But it's always that way: cities pay to build stadiums and arenas, further enriching owners.

The same thing happened in Columbus, Ohio. The Blue Jackets hockey team was losing $12 million a year so it threatened to leave town. The Columbus city council caved in, voting for $250 million in subsidies to the team despite its already rich owners.

In Detroit, by the way, the city council considered selling the Van Gogh and Rembrandt masterpieces in the Detroit Museum of Art to help solve the bankruptcy problem.

In America, money matters, not art for the ages, art that uplifts, stimulates and cheers so many people.

Sparks Tribune, Sept. 5, 2013

Getting away with murder

Paul Mitchell, a UNR journalism colleague and good friend, told me a story that I, a white guy, never forgot: he was once followed by a police car in New Jersey for "driving while black."

Most African-Americans have experienced something similar, something as humiliating and degrading.

Ask African-Americans followed by security guards while shopping. Ask the parents of Trayvon Martin, whose 17-year-old son was slain "walking while black" in a gated community in Sanford, Fla.

Martin's killer, George Zimmerman, was acquitted recently of second-degree murder and manslaughter in the February 2012 slaying. In the minds of the six women on the jury, Zimmerman was the victim, not the pursuer, not the stalker.

The verdict was a gross miscarriage of justice. As a Latina juror declared after the acquittal: Zimmerman "got away with murder" but she voted to acquit because of Florida law.

Martin, unarmed, a skinny kid and no threat to anyone, was walking with Skittles and iced tea. Zimmerman was a self-appointed community vigilante, a wannabe cop.

He was also an obsessive. He called 911 more than 40 times, often ranting about the "presence of frightening strangers." He had two run-ins with police because he couldn't control his temper.

In the Martin murder, Zimmerman shouted to a police dispatcher: "Shit, he's running!" The dispatcher asked: "Are you following him?" Yes. "We don't need you to do that," the dispatcher said.

But Zimmerman persisted in his mad pursuit. He began following Martin, first in his SUV then on foot. In the perfervid mind of Zimmerman, Martin was a "fucking coon," a "hoodie." (A hoodie? Naturally. It was a rainy night.)

Zimmerman, confronting Martin, asked that racist question: "What are you doing around here?"

Finally: a fight and a fatal shot.

Neighborhood Watch is a modern name for slave patrols. Slave patrols were groups of three to six white men who enforced discipline on slaves during the antebellum South. They policed the plantations and hunted fugitive slaves. The patrols started in South Carolina in 1704 and quickly spread throughout the South.

The national manual citing the code of conduct for Neighborhood Watch programs is emphatic: "Members do not possess police powers and they should not carry weapons or pursue vehicles." Zimmerman ignored that code.

However, the jury was instructed that under Florida law Zimmerman "had no duty to retreat and had the right to stand his ground and meet force with force, including deadly force if he reasonably believed that it was necessary to do so to prevent death or great bodily harm."

The verdict was predictable and inevitable. Southern "justice" is often a travesty. Florida's stand-your-ground law gives Rambos like Zimmerman an easy defense in settling domestic quarrels, road rage, bar fights and drug violence.

It allows citizens to take extraordinary steps to defend themselves when they feel threatened. Skin color is perceived as a threat. They make all black men suspects. They are licenses to kill.

Such outrageous laws should be abolished but they won't be. Florida, like some 20 other states with stand-your-ground laws, is a leader in the nation's gun-crazed culture. Last year alone Florida issued 173,000 new concealed-carry gun permits.

In 2012 police, security guards or vigilantes like Zimmerman killed 136 unarmed black men and women while monitoring people deemed a threat to white property and privilege.

Such laws allow hotheads to "shoot first and ask questions later," black columnist Eugene Robinson points out. And Jesse Jackson puts the Martin slaying in the proper perspective: racial profiling.

Michelle Alexander, civil rights advocate, attorney and author, said: "It is the Zimmerman mindset that must be found guilty, far more than the man himself. It is a mindset that views black men and boys as nothing but a threat, good for nothing, up to no good."

Blacks are aware, too, that courts are instruments of repression and oppression. Blacks are sentenced more harshly than whites for identical crimes. They serve far longer jail terms.

The murder of the innocent Trayvon Martin exemplifies the persistent racism in America, a nightmare that never ends. Social justice and human dignity remain elusive for blacks in this blatantly biased nation.

But perhaps one consolation for blacks: they get great support from liberal whites. As Nation magazine phrased it: "Thousands have marched, hundreds of thousands have signed petitions and millions have expressed their grief and outrage at the acquittal."

Typical of that outpouring was the reaction of a white woman friend of mine. When she heard the news she wept.

Sparks Tribune, Aug. 1, 2013

Racism haunts judicial system

Fifty years after the March on Washington for justice, freedom and jobs, African-Americans still do not get justice in drug sentencing, their freedom is curtailed by punitive prison terms and unemployment remains high.

The disparity in crime and punishment is cruel. Blacks are four times as likely than whites to be arrested on charges of marijuana possession. Blacks are six times more likely than whites to be incarcerated.

Black joblessness remains high at 12.6 percent. But among black young people between 18 and 29, the rate is an unconscionable 20.9 percent.

Clearly race is still divisive in America. It probably will still be on Doomsday.

The rage to punish is one of the many dark sides of America.

A 22-year-old black youth with no criminal record was sentenced to 45 years in prison for four sales of an eighth of an ounce of cocaine. Another black youth, 25, was sentenced to 20 years in prison for selling four grams of cocaine. It was his first offense.

Such sentencing is not just outrageous. It's inhuman.

Discriminatory sentencing accounts for swelling prison rolls.

Among vengeful sentencing and asinine laws are: mandatory minimum sentencing laws, tying the hands of judges; three-strikes-and-you're-out laws that imprison people for life even if the third felony is stealing a golf bag; and statutes that prohibit early release for good behavior.

Congress and state legislatures enacted tough-on-crime laws. Politicians passed these harsh laws because they did not want to go before voters appearing to be "soft on crime." Actually, they were tough-on-blacks laws.

Michelle Alexander, an Ohio State University law professor who has written passionately about the "New Jim Crow," laments "the millions of lives that have been wasted in the drug war and deeply misguided policies that have caused more harm and suffering than they have prevented."

This bogus war began in 1971 when President Nixon declared drug abuse "public enemy No. 1." Its cost has been in the trillions on federal and state levels.

Moreover, it has led to unconstitutional racial profiling: police targeting black citizens and black neighborhoods.

A federal district court in New York last week struck down stop-and-frisk laws. Judge Shira Sheindlin called the practice racially discriminatory, violating the equal protection clause of the 14th Amendment. Blacks were stopped, whites ignored.

Warehousing of inmates has led to an enormous growth in the private prison industry. The New Orleans Times-Picayune noted that more than half of Louisiana's 40,000 inmates are housed in prisons run by private companies.

Privatization madness leads to profit making in a non-profit responsibility of states. Prison companies spend millions on political campaign donations while lobbyists push for ever tougher state and federal crime legislation.

Other special interests are anxious to perpetuate the drug war. Police unions and police departments are dependent on federal funds to fulfill budgetary needs.

Pot should be legalized. Smoking pot should not even be a misdemeanor. Smoking a joint is harmless. The real drugs are cigarettes and alcohol.

President Obama ought to be out front on legalization of cannabis. He is term-limited so need not worry about alienating some voters. Yet he is retrograde on pot as he is on so much else, opposing state marijuana legalization and shutting medical clinics dispensing pot.

Yet look at how effective medical marijuana has been in relieving pain, nausea and vomiting caused by various diseases. Obama refuses to look let alone act sensibly.

America must get rid of its puritanical notion that pot is a drug and should be banned.

Washington state and Colorado decriminalized pot last fall. It's a tax windfall. Washington calculates it will reap $560 million annually for legalization of pot.

Drug treatment programs are essential. Taxing marijuana would produce funds for them. The Oakland Plan has been successful for three years with its 5 percent tax on cannabis-related sales.

The drug war must be ended if the nation is ever to achieve some degree of sanity about pot.

William Otis, who teaches at Georgetown law school, rightly considers continued criminalization of weed a never-ending bonanza for drug dealers. Their markup on the street is tremendous.

The solution is simple: legalize, tax and regulate the sale of marijuana on a national level. Replacing prohibition with taxation and regulation would provide needed revenue for strapped state and federal budgets.

As Truthout online has noted: "Marijuana is the linchpin of the drug war. Legalizing it will sound the death knell for this devastating crime against humanity."

Sparks Tribune, Aug. 22, 2013

Sex attacks sully military

The Pentagon recently revealed a double case of foxes guarding its chicken coops.

In one case an Army sergeant serving as sexual assault coordinator at Fort Hood in Texas is under investigation for sexual assault. In the other an Air Force lieutenant colonel in charge of preventing sexual assault has been arrested for feeling a woman's breasts and buttocks in a parking lot in Arlington, Va.

The cases illustrate the terrible problem the military faces in what Jaclyn Friedman calls America's culture of "toxic masculinity." Friedman, chief of Women, Action and the Media, explains: "Men are trained to think that the way to be a man is to have power over and to dehumanize women."

To call it "training" is exaggerated. But the military does have what the New York Times calls an "entrenched culture of sexual violence." According to an article in USA Today: "Male recruits are drawn from a society where violence and objectification of women are staple elements of films and video games."

And, yes, an Air Force brochure advises assault victims not to fight off attackers. The brochure, issued at the Shaw Air Force base in South Carolina, reads: "It may be advisable to submit rather than resist."

The Department of Defense (DOD) recently released a survey showing that 26,000 service members are assaulted annually. One of four women is attacked. The DOD estimates that 500 men and women are sexually assaulted every week--an incredible three an hour.

The Pentagon faces two huge obstacles: the great majority of sexual assault victims do not report the crimes out of fear of retribution and the absurdity of what the military calls justice.

Women usually will not report sex crimes because the attacker is often her commander. He can give her bad reports ending her military career. Women also fear that they will not get justice. They are right about that.

As Clemenceau, premier of France during World War I, observed: "Military justice is to justice what military music is to music." Military prosecution is the prerogative of commanders.

Just one example out of many similar cases: a co-worker raped a Navy aviation commander. The rapist was not prosecuted and the woman denied re-enlistment. As an old Latin expression says: "from this sample we may judge of the whole."

The victims are usually expelled on phony charges of "personality disorders" while the offenders go free. This injustice needs to be fixed by Congress--presuming the civilian government still rules the military.

Among other Pentagon problems:

• The United States spends more on the military than all other nations combined. (Calling it defense is a gross misuse of the word.)

• The U.S. military empire has 1,000 bases globally. Their presence in most cases is unnecessary. (America also finances three-quarters of military spending by NATO, an organization that ought to be abolished.)

• Congress whips up the military costs. Take a typical example: Rep. Howard McKeon of California. His 25th congressional district has a Navy weapons station, an Army fort, an Air Force base and a Marine site for mountain warfare training.

• Arms manufacturers lobby the Pentagon for more and more spending. Northrup Grumman has already spent $6 million on Congress this year. (Biggest arms maker beneficiary: Lockheed Martin, getting $30 billion annually.)

• Military waste in the military is incredible. Congress forces the Army to spend $436 million on tanks it doesn't want. But the Ohio congressional delegation insists. The tanks are built in Ohio. The Pentagon allowed a private firm providing food and water to U.S. troops in Afghanistan to overbill taxpayers $757 million. Yet it gave the company a no-bid contract extension worth $4 billion over three years.

America may be in Afghanistan for decades. Kabul wants Americans to stay well beyond the 2014 withdrawal date. A forever war.

Another endless war is that on terrorism. Congress gave a blank check for presidents to declare wars after 9/11.

An article in Nation magazine by Richard Kim deplored the presidential role on terrorism: "We suspend the Constitution and create government bureaucracies for espionage, covert operations and assassinations. Since 9/11 it has become a political imperative that our nation must go to any lengths to combat terrorism."

Yet America itself has often killed innocent victims with weapons of death and terror. Just a few of the many cases:

• Dropped atomic bombs on Hiroshima and Nagasaki.

• Hammered Afghan citizens with 1,228 cluster bombs.

• Endangered half the Iraq population with cancer because of tons of depleted uranium shells unleashed during the war. And, the senseless U.S. war rendered 14 percent of the population orphans.

• Spawned genocide in the "killing fields" of Southeast Asia, including the gratuitous release of 277 million cluster bombs on Laos.

Sparks Tribune, May 30, 2013

Senator thwarts women's justice

Committee members in the House and Senate get so attached to the subject their committee handles that they ignore the best interests of most people.

Take Senator Carl Levin of Michigan. This so-called liberal recently stripped from a defense bill any reference to curbs on sexual assault in the military. Levin is chairman of the Armed Services Committee so he can do as he pleases even if it means trampling on justice.

Senator Kristen Gillibrand of New York wanted to give military prosecutors rather than commanders the power to decide whether to try sexual assault cases. Her aim: increase the number of women and men who report sexual assaults without fear of retaliation by commanders.

Levin says no. He's boss. Yet it's hardly a democracy when one man out of 315 million Americans can decide what the law should be.

Levin is a long-time supporter of the military even when it is wrong. So he stacks the deck, compiling a witness list of people who support keeping sexual assault in the chain of military command.

The terrible problem of sexual assault on women and men be damned. Levin is the Lone Great Decider.

"It is the chain of command that must be held accountable if it fails to change a military culture," Levin pontificates.

That says it all: military culture, a rape culture, a culture that badly needs to be destroyed.

War hawk nominated

President Obama continues to name the wealthy and the warmongers to major positions and as his advisers. The latest Obama appointment: Susan Rice as national security adviser, the personification of a war hawk.

"Rice's willingness to utter demonstrable falsehoods to

defend actions by the United States is troubling," Stephen Zunes of Truthout says.

Even more troubling is her eagerness to have the nation go to war. She urged war in Iraq despite the judgment of analysts and investigative reporters repudiating the lies told by President G.W. Bush.

Rice cried out: "It's clear that Iraq poses a major threat." She made this claim despite the fact that Iraq jettisoned chemical and biological weapons and disbanded its nuclear program.

When Secretary of State Colin Powell libeled Iraq with false claims, Rice exclaimed: "Powell proved that Iraq had those weapons and is hiding them."

Her openness to still another war in the Middle East was obvious last fall when she announced that "there is no daylight" between America and the Israeli government of Benjamin Netanyahu pushing for an attack on Iran because of its nuclear program. (Israeli supporters never mention Israel's nuclear capability.)

Congress flunks test

Debt on college student loans is $1 trillion a year. The average is $40,000 per student. Yet Congress allowed the student loan interest to double to 6.8 percent effective Monday.

Congress should be doing everything to increase college ranks instead of discouraging enrollment. But that's the congressional way: encourage business while abandoning people who most need help.

Big banks get loans from the Federal Reserve at the fantastic rate of 0.75 percent.

College education should be free as it once was in California. But the federal government will make $51 billion from student loans this year. Next year: double that.

Harry Reid once again proved his piss-poor leadership.

Reid, Senate majority leader from Nevada, refused to consider a bipartisan plan to keep the interest rate temporarily at 3.4 percent, wrongly calling it "a Republican solution."

Snowden not guilty

The government has charged Edward Snowden with violating the Espionage Act and stealing government property to disclose classified information. Not guilty.

He courageously did the American people a tremendous favor by leaking classified documents of the National Security Agency. Ever since the Vietnam War we learned that governments, whether Democratic or Republican, should never be believed unless they provide convincing evidence to the contrary.

As that magnificent columnist I.F. Stone pointed out decades ago: "All governments are run by liars."

The government classifies an unbelievable amount of information that need not be classified. But governments have a dark desire for secrecy. Obama promised openness but he's just as secretive.

Snowden was lifting the veil on the surveillance by the National Security Agency. He did not harm the government any more than other important leakers like Bradley Manning and Julian Assange did. The leakers are merely telling the truth.

European officials were enraged that the NSA bugged European Union offices in Brussels, Washington and New York, installing listening devices and tapping into computer networks. Snowden leaks also revealed that NSA gathers information on millions of American phone calls.

It's "turnkey tyranny," Nation magazine rightly calls it.

Sparks Tribune, July 4, 2013

Grim cigarette graphics needed

No one should smoke. The lesson has been hammered home again and again and again.

The latest lesson comes from the European Parliament, voting to increase the size of warning labels on cigarette packs and pointing out that e-cigarettes and flavored cigarettes are just as dangerous.

But those measures are not enough. What is needed are the graphic warning labels the Congress authorized the Food and Drug Administration to print four years ago. Unfortunately, the FDA was stymied in court.

One warning label showed a toe tag on a corpse. In another, a mother blew smoke in her baby's face. In yet another, next to the grim message, "WARNING: cigarettes cause cancer," an ashen-faced woman lies dying in a hospital bed.

Most graphic and most gruesome of all: "WARNING: cigarettes are addictive." Alongside is a picture of a man puffing away--exhaling smoke from a hole in his chest.

Nevertheless, the noisome work of the tobacco industry is constantly being glamorized by deceptive advertising despite the fact that 700,000 Europeans and 440,000 Americans die annually from smoking-related illnesses.

Words, words, words

Most governing bodies in the United States stop debate with a simple majority vote. Not in the U.S. Senate, hag-ridden by the filibuster.

It prevents essential measures such as immigration reform and gun control. It enthrones the tyranny of the minority.

Dennis Myers, news editor of the Reno News & Review, wrote an extensive backgrounder in a cover story for the Reno News & Review in 2009. It was aptly titled "The World's Greatest Dysfunctional Body."

Myers, the most thorough and deepest Nevada journalist, summed up his argument: "The Senate has become a parliamentary skull and bones, worshipping pointless ritual rather than serving the public's needs. The senators are playing sanity-challenged parliamentary games."

Senate Majority Leader Harry Reid of Nevada can do something about it but he won't. When he first ran for the Senate in 1986 he opposed the filibuster, calling it crazy.

Now? He favors the filibuster. But constant vows to change the rules are hollow.

Every time Republican obstructionists thwart President Obama's judicial or governmental nominees, Reid flashes justifiable anger. So he threatens to get a 51-vote majority to adopt the "nuclear option" of abolishing the filibuster's 60-vote rule.

"Something has to change and I hope we can make the changes necessary," he says.

Actually he fears that if Democrats lose control of the Senate they need the filibuster as a "veto." So Reid issues words, words, words, pious hopes for cooperation, but never any action.

Spying on allies

U.S. spying on Germany, France, Mexico and Brazil justifiably angered government leaders of the four nations, all staunch supporters of America.

The National Security Agency siphoned off emails and text messages of Brazilian President Dilma Rousseff. The outrageous behavior of NSA included eavesdropping on the cellphone of German Chancellor Angela Merkel.

No wonder the U.S. government wants to prosecute and persecute Edward Snowden whose harvest of documents exposed the out-of-control, mad careening of NSA.

Chains make billions

Pay at fast food chains is so low that millions of employees get $7 billion a year in welfare benefits, a study by a labor economist at the University of California, Berkeley, reveals.

"The median wage for these workers is $8.65 an hour," Professor Ken Jacobs says. "Only 13 percent have health benefits through their employer. The combination of low wages, meager benefits and often part-time work means that many families of fast food workers must rely on taxpayer-funded safety-net programs to makes ends meet."

Meanwhile, the largest fast food chains make more than $15 billion in profits. The villains: McDonalds, Pizza Hut, Taco Bell, KFC, Subway, Burger King, Wendy's, Dunkin' Donuts, Dairy Queen, Little Caesar's and Domino's.

Tweeter self-destructs

It is hard to imagine why any government official would post anything damaging to himself on Twitter. Hubris? Stupidity? Whatever the reason that official deserves to be fired.

Such is the case of Jofi Joseph. During the day he was a White House staffer working on national security. At night he mused on Twitter about foreign policy, the lack of intelligence of his colleagues and his obsession with the appearance of women.

For two years Joseph thought he was writing anonymously. But White House staffers got suspicious because his Twitter postings showed insider knowledge. After a White House investigation, he was canned, his promising career ended.

White House sleuths "parsed more than 2,000 tweets," according to Politico, checking out Joseph's shopping, travels and conversations to uncover the high-profile idiot.

One more time: there is no privacy on social media.

Sparks Tribune, Nov. 14, 2013

Congress, taxes and 'dark money'

Tim Cook, Apple CEO, recently charmed Senate panelists so sweetly that his corporation's tax avoidance became a wonderful thing rather than the outrage it is.

Here was the fiery Sen. Carl Levin of Michigan, bowing and scraping before the huge tax evader while holding aloft an Apple app like a happy consumer.

"We love the iPhone and iPad," chairman Levin exulted at a hearing held by the investigations committee. As the New York Times reported: "The big cats on the committee were practically eating out of Cook's hand."

Apple avoided paying billions in taxes to the Treasury while creating "ghost companies" abroad. It's part of an even bigger picture: multinationals based in America hold more than $1.6 trillion in cash invested overseas--funds taxable at 35 percent in this country.

Apple created Apple Operations International incorporated in Ireland. But it keeps its bank accounts in America and holds board meetings in California. The real scandal in the U.S. tax code is that corporations like Apple get away scot-free--with the approval of Congress.

Meanwhile, the supposed IRS targeting of the Tea Party and conservative spinoffs caused a hullabaloo. But the uproar was unwarranted. The IRS was checking any group applying for a special tax status to see if they were engaged in political activity.

"Organizations of all persuasions were pulled in," outgoing acting IRS commissioner Steve Miller testified. "Only 70 of the 300 organizations were Tea Party groups."

The IRS has interpreted tax laws to allow big corporations and wealthy individuals to make secret campaign donations through political fronts called "social welfare organizations" like Karl Rove's "Crossroads."

And that is the result of the Citizens United decision by a reactionary Supreme Court. The ruling led to a cascade of "dark money" in politics. As always, money rules, not wise policies and leveling of the mountain of inequality.

(Cook's pay package? Poor fellow. He makes only $1.36 million in salary and $2.8 million in bonus incentives. And, yes, he gets 1 million shares of Apple stock.)

Warren for president

Social media gossip has anointed Hillary Clinton as the nation's first woman president. But a far better choice in the 2016 election would be Senator Elizabeth Warren of Massachusetts.

Warren first came to public attention as an advocate of a federal financial protection bureau and chair of the congressional oversight panel on the economy. After Congress enacted the Economic Stabilization Act in 2010 she advised President Obama on implementing it.

She was such a staunch battler for the consumer that advocacy groups urged the president to name her the first head of the Consumer Financial Protection Bureau. But Obama, born without a backbone, refused. He was convinced Warren could not be confirmed because of Republican fears that she would represent people not business.

The fears were justified. But Obama should have fought for the best, not pick the third-rater he did. It would be wonderful irony if such a refusal led to the first woman president.

If elected, Elizabeth Warren would be the first people's president since FDR. Hillary Clinton would be a middle-of-the-roader just as President Clinton was and President Obama is.

Here's an example of how Warren would fight for the people. The interest rate for new student loans is due to double to 6.8 percent July 1. Banks have a rate of 0.75.

"Why should the big banks get a nearly free ride while people trying to get an education pay nine times more?" the Massachusetts senator asks. "The federal government is profiting off loans to our young people while giving a far better deal to the same Wall Street banks that crashed the economy and destroyed millions of jobs."

Warren has introduced a bill allowing students to borrow money at the same rate as the biggest banks. Alas, it perished in committee as most sensible measures do.

Our gutless PBS

PBS has long provided the best news and political commentary in American. But it, like the corporate media, lacks courage.

It refused to run the documentary "Citizen Koch" for fear of offending billionaire industrialist David Koch. Koch has given $23 million to PBS.

Killing the hard-hitting documentary undercuts the integrity of PBS. It also points up the need for much greater congressional funding, which spends far less per capita on public broadcasting than most wealthy nations do.

It's a question of values that America so often so woefully lacks.

Sparks Tribune, June 6, 2013

Religion invades public schools

Despite the ruling of the Supreme Court that there must be a rigid separation of church and state, regressive states insist on dragging religion into public schools.

A high school in Jackson, Ohio, has a devotional painting of Jesus, "The Head of Christ," hanging in the hall students pass to enter the cafeteria. In Mississippi Gov. Phil Bryant signed a bill allowing schools to pray over school intercoms and at assemblies, graduations and sports events.

Mike Huckabee, former governor of Arkansas and a minister, approves of churches and schools blending.

"We ask why there is violence in our schools but we have systematically removed God from our schools," Huckabee says. "Should we be surprised that schools would become places of carnage?"

Removal of God from schools has nothing to do with violence.

The Mississippi measure is corrosive and unconstitutional. But none of that matters in the hinterlands of Mississippi and 23 other reactionary states that have Republican governors and GOP control of legislatures.

The McCollum ruling by the Supreme Court in 1948 struck down religious instruction in Champaign, Ill., as a violation "of personal conscience." It declared that the "wall between church and state must be kept high and impregnable."

But, really, why should states feel compelled to keep religion out of schools when U.S. Treasury coins and bills proclaim "In God we trust"?

That unconstitutional message was cemented in 1864 after the Rev. M.R. Watkinson of Ridleyville, Pa., wrote to Treasury Secretary Salmon Chase declaring the slogan essential to "relieve us of the ignominy of heathenism."

Nothing ignominious about unbelief. Many Americans support the Freedom from Religion Foundation suit demanding that the government drop the slogan.

If justice prevails, it will win. But justice often doesn't prevail. In 2011 a retrograde Supreme Court rejected a similar plea.

Where's the outrage?

President Obama is packing his second-term Cabinet with the likes of Jacob Lew. Lew, new treasury secretary, got a $685,000 gift from New York University when he resigned as executive secretary in 2006 to take a job with Citigroup.

Lew resigned voluntarily. NYU was under no contract obligation to give him severance pay. Why should a tax-exempt university give him an enormous exit bonus?

He was hired as executive VP in 2001. Some years he made $840,000. He also received mortgages of $1.5 million from the school as a perk, $440,000 of which it forgave.

NYU is a private university so it is free to dole out largesse. But even the rich donors cannot be pleased.

Am I the only one in America outraged? Certainly the editors of the august New York Times were not, burying the story on page 17.

Sen. Chuck Grassley of Iowa was unhappy about the giveaway. Grassley, former chairman of the Senate Finance Committee, said:

"The problem of colleges that find money for executive suites even as they raise tuition is not unique to New York University. NYU is among the most expensive, has a well-funded endowment and high student debt loads. It should explain how its generous treatment of Lew abets its educational mission."

University officials said it is "not uncommon for large corporations to make payments to senior officials on their departure." But one consultant countered that it was unusual to get "a ton of money" for voluntary departure.

It's more than unusual. It's an outrage.

Oust Spanish royals

As the Enlightenment apostle Diderot remarked: "Men will never be free until the last king is strangled with the entrails of the last priest."

Certainly Spain is not free.

Its King Juan Carlos has vast personal wealth. He stashes the filthy lucre he inherited from his father in secret Swiss bank accounts. Yet Juan Carlos came to the throne in 1975 with almost no money.

The monarchy costs Spanish taxpayers 8 million euros a year ($12 million), supporting the king, his wife, children and grandchildren in regal style. The expenditure is hardly justifiable at any time, let alone now with Spanish austerity hurting most people and Spain's economy pinched.

Thousands of Spaniards demonstrated against the king on a recent Sunday in Madrid, the 82nd anniversary of the last republican government. (That government was ousted by the Franco dictatorship after a gruesome civil war.)

The Spanish Socialist Party demands that parliament provide detailed information about the king's personal finances. But that is warm beer.

What they should be demanding is abolition of the monarchy as the British Labor Party did about royalty in the enlightened days of Laborites.

Sparks Tribune, April 25, 2013

61

NRA, Reid foil gun law reform

The National Rifle Association will not allow even the most anemic steps toward gun control.

The sad fact is that the NRA rules, not Congress, when guns are the issue. No lobby in America is more powerful, not even the vaunted Jewish drumbeaters.

The NRA mobilized its four million members to flood the Senate with phone calls, emails and letters. It spent $500,000 in advertising on the day of the Senate vote. (The ads made the lying claim that President Obama seeks to ban guns). The NRA dispensed $800,000 in campaign contributions (bribes) to members of Congress.

NRA spokesman Wayne LaPierre urged putting armed guards in schools. "The only thing that stops a bad guy with a gun is a good guy with a gun," LaPierre declared, uttering typical NRA claptrap.

The Senate quickly forgot the Connecticut Sandy Hook massacre in December: 20 kids and five educators slaughtered by a gunman with an assault weapon.

So it naturally defeated nine recent proposals to restore sanity to gun laws. It rejected bans on assault weapons and high-capacity magazines. It rejected efforts to expand background checks on gun purchasers.

All failed to get the 60 votes needed in the bipartisan agreement before the voting. And that's the problem. Sen. Majority Leader Harry Reid of Nevada talks a good game, lamenting defeat of measures "that 90 percent of Americans agree on."

But he is the villain behind Senate rejection. He refuses to abandon the filibuster. A majority should rule in a democracy, not a supermajority.

Moreover, rural states have inordinate power because of having two senators while urban states with far more people have just two senators. Columnist E.J. Donne points out that it is theoretically possible for 41 senators representing *just 11 percent* of the nation's population to block any bill.

Andrew Cohen of the Brennan Center for Justice deplores "the widespread failure of the media to adequately describe the nature of the filibuster requiring a supermajority vote for any contentious issue." (Essential immigration reform could be the next measure to fail in the antidemocratic Senate.) Cohen calls the filibuster what it is: a self-inflicted wound.

There are plenty of other villains behind Senate failure. Gun manufacturers like Smith & Wesson, Remington and Glock make enormous amounts of money and donate heavily to the NRA.

Another: the Internet provides easy access for criminals to get guns. The New York Times reported: "One widely popular Website contains tens of thousands of private postings of gun sales. Many buyers and sellers were killers."

Another villain is the influential Sen. Tom Coburn of Oklahoma who expressed an unfounded fear that "stricter background checks would create a national gun registry."

Still other villains are the states that have slashed $1.6 billion from mental health programs since 2009.

Gabrielle Giffords, former House representative from Arizona and shooting victim, noted: "a minority of senators gave into fear and blocked commonsense legislation that would have made it harder for criminals and people with dangerous mental illnesses to get hold of deadly firearms."

The Supreme Court is hardly blameless. In its 2008 ruling in District of Columbia v. Heller it held that the Second Amendment protects an individual's right to bear arms for self-defense in the home. It affirmed a decision by the Court of Appeals for the D.C. Circuit which ruled unconstitutional a D.C. law requiring rifles and shotguns to be unloaded and disassembled--or restrained by a trigger lock.

In dissent, Justice Stevens, joined by Justices Ginsburg, Souter and Breyer, called the majority judgment "strained and unpersuasive" in overturning longstanding precedent.

Breyer said the court "bestowed a dramatic upheaval in the law." He pointed out that the Founders' reference to colonial militia in the Second Amendment made it clear they were referring to today's equivalent of national guards.

After the Senate crushed all efforts at gun control, survivors of killings at Virginia Tech and mass shootings in Arizona, shouted from the Senate gallery: "Shame on you." An angry President Obama echoed those sentiments by calling the vote a "shameful day for Washington."

A terrible fact is that so many Americans love, cherish and possess guns. One out of five American adults own guns--about 50 million people. The national gun culture is deeply engrained: 270 Americans are shot every day.

No wonder the United States refuses to join civilized nations that curb deadly use of firearms. America is a land of violence.

Sparks Tribune, May 2, 2013

Sobs no cure for gun woes

The probability that we may fall in the struggle ought not to deter us from the support of a cause we believe to be just.

Lincoln in film "Lincoln"

President Obama's first statement on the Connecticut massacre of 20 kids was a tear-filled declaration that "our hearts are broken." Nothing about gun controls.

After a Colorado shooting massacre in July, Obama expressed a pious hope: "This is a day for prayer and reflection…May the Lord bring comfort and healing." Nothing about gun controls.

Obama, despite his overwhelming re-election, remains a follower not a leader. He declines to take on the powerful NRA.

After the Aurora, Colo., killings he did not call for a ban on assault weapons or high capacity bullet clips. He refused to do anything about easy gun accessibility. He refused to urge laws making it difficult for psychotics to possess guns. He refused to urge monitoring of sales at gun shows.

Finally, four days after the disaster in Newtown, Conn., and six months after the Colorado tragedy, he decided to do something about gun madness.

Good. Better to fight and lose rather than constantly compromise on issues as he did during his first term.

Obama faults the nation for not doing enough "to keep our children safe from harm." Yet he himself is egregious for failing to do anything about it.

Sobs and handwringing are not enough.

As Robert Parry of the online Consortium News wrote, when the Founders wrote the Second Amendment they could not envision modern weaponry mowing down children.

Brubeck's 'Take Five'

The New York Times publishes obituaries of people who "don't die" anywhere else. That is, the obits deal with people prominent in their fields but are unheard of by a vast majority of readers.

However, the Times obits of famous people are given such fine treatment that the articles are sometimes clipped and saved because they are full of facts, quotations and anecdotes.

Such a one was accorded Dave Brubeck, a giant of jazz who died recently. His "Time Out" was the first jazz album to sell a million copies. The centerpiece of that album was "Take Five," an irresistible work. My three young daughters danced to its lively rhythms.

As the Times put it: "Brubeck brought a distinctive mix of experimentation and accessibility that won over listeners."

Brubeck scorned racism.

In the 1950s he dismissed suggestions by college deans that asked him not to perform with a racially mixed band (his bassist, Gene Wright, was black). He refused to tour South Africa in 1958 because it demanded that his band be all white.

During a tour in the Mideast and India for the State Department, his quintet didn't stick to 4/4 time, what Brubeck called march-style jazz. He turned to the enormously popular 5/4 time.

"One of the reasons I believe in jazz is that the oneness of man can come through the heart," Brubeck said. "It's the same any place in the world--that heartbeat."

Obscene Chinese wealth

The family of Chinese Premier Wen Jiabao has amassed a $2.7 billion fortune. A Chinese foreign ministry spokesman said the report "blackens China's name."

Indeed it does. The very essence of communism, once espoused by China, barred such obscenity.

Labor hero dies

Ben Reiter of Sports Illustrated called the baseball Hall of Fame "a gated community maintained for the oligarchy" in its refusal to enroll Marvin Miller.

Miller, who died recently, gave the players free agency--an incredible liberation, breaking their chains and giving them more of what they are worth.

Unsung sports writer

Dave Zirin is the best sociological sportswriter in America. Zirin, Nation columnist, tells the often sordid truth about sports.

But he also tells heartwarming stories of courageous athletes who go against the grain of homophobia in sports. He cites boxer Orlando Cruz--boxing, the most macho of sports.

"Cruz has dealt a mighty blow to the stereotype that strength, bravery and toughness are heterosexual traits," Zirin writes. "He embodies a set of universal values we'd all do well to emulate."

Zirin also denounces Israel's destruction--twice--of a 10,000-seat soccer stadium in Palestine, once in 2006 and once this year.

Not just for the hell of it. But deliberately and willfully because "sports is more than loved in Gaza. It is an expression of humanity for those living under occupation."

"Attacking the athletic infrastructure is about attacking the idea that joy, normalcy or a universally recognizable humanity could ever be a part of life for Palestinians," Zirin writes. "Attacking sports is nothing less than killing hope. Unfortunately, Israel's total war is underwritten by the United States."

Sparks Tribune, Dec. 20, 2012

Outrage over Redskins name
silly political correctness

What's in a name? that which we call a rose / By
any other name would smell as sweet.
"Romeo and Juliet"

Sports columnists and TV commentators, wanting to show their righteous rage over racism, are howling over the nickname of Washington's National Football League team.

But the nickname, Redskins, is hardly a pejorative like racist names of yesteryear: "spic," "wop," "dago," "kike" and "nigger." The outrage over Redskins is political correctness run amok.

The picture of the Native American on the Redskins' helmet is dignified and noble. NFL Commissioner Roger Goodell rightly says the nickname "stands for pride and respect." Daniel Snyder, owner of the Redskins, calls it a badge of honor. Snyder makes two salient points:

• A poll of 1,000 Native Americans concluded that nine of 10 did not find the nickname offensive.

• The Richmond (Va.) Times Dispatch interviewed three leaders of Native American tribes in Virginia. None said he was offended by the name.

Snyder might have made another point: the very name Oklahoma comes from Choctaw words for red people: okla (people) and humma (red).

The clincher in the argument comes from Professor Grant Leneaux, dear friend of long standing at the University of Nevada, Reno.

He is a sensitive intellectual. If anyone would be offended by the word Redskins it would be Leneaux. He has Native American blood in his veins (Delaware) and is fiercely proud of the fact. Yet he says of the nickname: "It doesn't bother me.'

Hockey needs no mayhem

Hockey is a game of skill. It should ban fighting and body checking. They are mayhems, not skills.

Researchers at the Mayo Clinic in Rochester, Minn., recently confirmed what has long been obvious: hockey causes brain trauma and concussions, marring an exciting game.

Two National Hockey League players recently left games on a stretcher. One suffered a concussion. The other was knocked unconscious after being crunched from behind.

"Both were grotesque, asinine hits that we see with too much regularity," hockey writer Ross McKeon declares. "Scoring goals is always far better than fighting or dangerous hits."

Mossbacks argue that to end fighting and body checking would ruin the game. But that's nonsense. No loss of excitement resulted after youth hockey and college hockey barred fighting. USA Hockey and Hockey Canada upped the age of body checking to 13 after learning that body checking had caused alarming injuries to 11 and 12 year olds.

The Mayo Clinic reports that repeated hits to the head in NFL fights cause great harm to players. Left and right hooks lead to concussions.

Anyone who starts a fight in the NHL should be ejected immediately. Fighting should also draw long-term suspensions. The "great game" will flourish without concussions in fights and checks.

DH rule wrong

The American League is at a disadvantage in the World Series because of its policy of having a designated hitter. The National League has no DH.

In the World Series just completed, three of the games were played in the St. Louis Cardinals' ballpark. In those games the Boston Red Sox had to keep one of its best sluggers on the bench.

The DH was instituted in 1973 to provide more hits, more runs and more fan excitement. But as Dan Hinxman, sports editor of the Reno Gazette-Journal, points out, the DH kills late-game strategy.

"I prefer the National League game because managers have to figure out when to use pinch hitters and how to use their bullpen pitchers," Hinxman says.

I agree. The American League should revert to old-fashioned baseball by abolishing the DH. Pitchers should bat. The best ones learn how to bunt well, advancing runners.

(Yes, I know, the Red Sox won--and deservedly so--despite the disadvantage. Bosox designated hitter David Ortiz was magnificent with 11 hits in 16 at-bats. But my point remains.)

Sparks Tribune, Oct. 31, 2013

Labor law stacks deck

Labor desperately needs the Employee Free Choice Act, a law that would allow workers to unionize and bargain collectively if the majority in a unit sign up for it.

But as labor law now stands, workers have to vote to approve a union. This allows companies to intimidate, threaten and fire workers who lead organizing drives. Workers are fired for such trivial reasons as affixing names of the "wrong candidates" on their bumper stickers.

Companies also hold meetings for "political persuasion," meaning to "persuade" workers to vote "correctly."

Workers also face an insurmountable barrier: chains like Starbucks, Costco and Walmart are so popular despite their anti-union stances that a right-wing Congress will never enact a sign-up law.

Starbucks prospers because the demand for a coffee fix is tremendous. Costco and Walmart thrive because their prices are "right": low.

The low cost for shoppers takes a toll on the workers. Pay is so low at Walmart that in some cases employees qualify for government subsidy.

"Almost a quarter of all jobs in America now pay wages below the poverty line for a family of four," columnist Robert Reich points out. He cites particularly big-box retailers like Walmart.

As for Starbucks, Nation magazine labor writer Josh Eidelson observes: "While it cultivates a progressive image, Starbucks is overwhelmingly nonunion. It has repeatedly demonstrated its commitment to remain so."

The National Labor Relations Board ruled in 2009 that Starbucks had illegally fired four union leaders. But the case is on appeal, probably meaning appeal until the workers lose.

Workers also suffer under proliferating two-tier plans. Under it employers are reducing the pay of new hires as long as the pay of existing employees is not touched.

Even the country's most powerful unions have agreed to this unfairness on the false theory that it's better than no job at all.

Justice errs

Justice Sonia Sotomayor votes right on the Supreme Court but her judgment off the bench is faulty.

PepsiCo, giant beverage firm, is sponsoring a conference in April for women who attended Yale. Sotomayor, a graduate of Yale law school, is scheduled to speak.

"I didn't go to Pepsi University," one Yale degree holder said. Moreover, she deplored the company's public health record. (Food Safety News reported that Pepsi contains traces of a chemical that causes cancer in lab animals.)

Another grad, long-time critic of PepsiCo's ties with Yale, complained about Pepsi having "tentacles deep into Yale."

The idealists are right. But money is more important to universities than values.

Idiot law, idiot ruling

A Vancouver, Canada, man who won a fantasy football league prize of tickets and an all-expenses trip to the Super Bowl, couldn't collect. U.S. customs officials denied him entry at the Toronto airport because of a minor marijuana conviction in 1981.

Myles Wilkinson was 19 when he was caught with two grams of pot (about the weight of a paper clip). No wonder Wilkinson said he couldn't believe he was turned back "for something that happened 32 years ago."

But Dana Larsen is not surprised. Larsen, head of a Canadian group urging legalization of marijuana, says it happens all the time in Canada.

"Being a cannabis user should not be a criminal offense," Larsen said. "It should be regulated, taxed and controlled but not banned."

Voters in two U.S. states, Washington and Colorado, agreed in November elections. Perhaps five decades from now the Canadian and U.S. governments will also come to their senses about pot.

Dictator rules Russia

The Russian judiciary does the bidding of President "czar" Putin so it is hardly surprising a district court in Moscow recently placed an opposition leader under house arrest. He is Sergei Udaltsov, leader of the socialist movement, passionate public speaker and grandson of a staunch Bolshevik.

Udaltsov is under criminal charges of conspiracy to incite "mass" disorder. Doubtless he will be sentenced to 10 years in jail under Putin's KGB reign.

Putin's regime is also trying to prosecute Sergei Magnitsky, whistleblowing lawyer who died in a Moscow jail three years ago. He was jailed for investigating hundreds of millions of dollars stolen by Russian officials.

Magnitsky was beaten in jail and denied medical care, damaging Russia's image abroad.

Czar Putin couldn't care less.

Stan the Man

Stan Musial was one of baseball's greatest hitters with a lifetime average of .331. Musial, who died recently, played all 22 big league seasons with the St. Louis Cardinals (1941 to 1963).

Preacher Roe, a great pitcher of the era, advised pitchers facing Musial: "Throw him four wide ones and then pick him off first."

Sparks Tribune, Feb. 21, 2013

Protecting 'sacred' institutions

The pedophilia scandals over the past decade have a common seamy thread: institutions protect their reputations at the expense of children.

The Roman Catholic Church became notorious for pedophilia by priests. Coach Joe Paterno and Penn State officials covered up serial pedophilia. Newly released "perversion files" of the Boy Scouts reveal decades of "a corrosive culture of secrecy" that failed to protect kids.

Now we learn that the venerated BBC of Britain protected sexual abuse of 200 teenage girls in hospitals and children's homes by the late TV personality, Jimmy Savile.

The BBC abandoned an investigation of Savile, sullying an ethical reputation solidly built up for 50 years.

Prairie populist

George McGovern was no saint. No politician ever is. But he was a man of conscience.

"He taught us to stand up for human decency and honesty no matter what the cost," social critic Chris Hedges writes.

That cost was a trouncing as the Democratic candidate for president in 1972.

McGovern opposed the Vietnam War and urged the withdrawal of American forces in Indochina. He wisely told the Senate: "Every senator in this chamber is partly responsible for sending 50,000 young Americans to an early grave. This chamber reeks of blood."

So it did. But his was that voice in the wilderness.

McGovern, who died recently, declared that he wanted to "support our troops" by bringing them home. And he pointed out another truth: "I'm sick and tired of old men dreaming up wars in which young men do the dying."

Unfortunately in America this South Dakota prairie populist was a hopeless idealist in his quest for social justice and end to U.S. militarism.

Civilized nation

The socialist government of France constantly shames the blindness and puritanism of the U.S. Congress.

France's House has approved legislation to reimburse abortion expenses and to make contraception free for minors. French national medical insurance already pays for abortions for minors and the poor. Other women are reimbursed up to 80 percent for the $600 cost of an abortion.

The House measure, expected to pass the Senate, would make all abortions free and pay for contraception for those between 15 and 18.

King defies poverty

Spain is mired in such economic woes and poverty that many Spaniards are forced to rummage through garbage for food scraps. Yet the Spanish monarch, Juan Carlos I, dashes off on a pricey African safari.

It is unclear whether Juan Carlos is a millionaire or billionaire. But he does have an island home, yachts and scores of luxury automobiles.

One caustic Tweeter message summed up public outrage: "The Spaniards in slippers and the king with 70 cars."

Diderot, as long ago as the Enlightenment, was right: "Man will never be free until the last king is strangled with the entrails of the last priest."

Rape in Okinawa

Two Navy sailors stationed in Okinawa were charged recently with rape. Nothing new about U.S. military rapes there. But it raises the question once again: why does America even have bases on Okinawa 67 years after World War II?

Czar Putin

Russia revels in autocratic regimes: czars, Soviets and now President Putin.

The press under Putin is neither independent nor free, has little free speech, human rights are a joke and dissenters are jailed.

But the Putin czardom does have millionaires and billionaires, contrary to the socialist goal of equality.

Muslim rage

The most progressive publication in America is The Nation. This paragraph from a recent editorial shows it:

"The deepest wellsprings of resentment lie in U.S. policy in the Muslin world. From backing dictatorships, to the strangulation by sanctions and evisceration of Iraq, to drone strikes across Islamic nations, to steadfast support for Israel's occupation of Palestine now in its fifth decade, the list of grievances is long."

3 cheers for Chávez

The corporate media is on the wrong side as usual. It rooted for the defeat of President Chávez in his smashing re-election triumph although he has reduced income inequality in Venezuela to its lowest level in Latin America.

Chávez cut poverty by 70 percent while greatly expanding aid to health, education and housing.

Brave teacher

A high school English teacher in Knoxville, Tenn., did exactly what advisers of student publications should be doing: flouting community thinking.

The teacher, James Yoakley, approved the publication of a yearbook story, "It's OK to be gay," and signed off on an article in the student newspaper by an atheist explaining her lack of belief.

His wisdom was rewarded with demotion to middle school.

Aperçu

Presidents come and presidents go but Shakespeare abideth forever.

Sparks Tribune, Nov. 8, 2012

Homophobic law, patriarch's approval

Russia and President Putin have gone backwards on gay rights, suppressing homosexuality with a law crushing human dignity.

Euphemism masks the law. Putin says it "protects children" by banning "propaganda on nontraditional sexual relationships." But no one is fooled.

Homophobia runs deep in Russia. Eighty-six percent of its people strongly disapprove of homosexuality. The country harasses LGBTs on the street, intimidating and arresting them.

Patriarch Kirill 1, head of the Russian Orthodox Church, heartily approves of the Putin-parliament decree. He decries gay and lesbian relationships and says same-sex marriage portends "a very dangerous sign of the apocalypse."

It's not only a gross exaggeration. Once again a Christian acts unchristian.

Anyone training to be a priest should be compelled to read the moving, short book two of Hugo's huge novel, "Les Misérables." Bishop Myriel will teach priests-to-be what it is to act like a Christian.

The new law ignited international condemnation. Some people called for a boycott of the Winter Olympics at Sochi, Russia, in February.

Such outrage is justified but the proposed solution is not. Boycotts just punish the world's greatest athletes and the countless people enthralled by the games on TV.

However, the International Olympic Committee should not hold the games in nations that violate civil and human rights.

Low wages prompt protests

Fast-food workers, fed up with low pay that requires a second job to make ends meet, have cried enough. They walked off their jobs in 60 cities Labor Day weekend. They also protested erratic schedules, lack of job security, miserable working conditions and lack of benefits.

In Chicago, workers took to the streets with T-shirts demanding $15 an hour. This may seem excessive to some people since it is twice the minimum wage. But one worker at a Wendy's in Chicago, making $8.25 an hour, calls his pay "impossible to live on."

"I'm a father, a husband," he declares. "I'm always robbing Peter to pay Paul."

Corporate McDonald's is unfazed. It issued a moral lecture, declaring that wise use of money would balance budgets better.

John Mason, political science professor at William Patterson University in New Jersey, says the McDonald's pay is "30 percent below the official poverty line." He adds: "The five largest employers in the U.S., including Walmart and McDonald's, all pay a niggardly wage."

A report by economists Lawrence Mishel and Heidi Shierholz, "A Decade of Flat Wages," declares "the vast majority of U.S. workers, including white-collar and blue-collar workers and those with or without a college degree, have endured more than a decade of wage stagnation."

McDonald's CEO? He makes $13.8 million a year "toiling" for the Golden Arches.

Congress lauds status quo

Congress has hailed the "new policies" recently announced by the Pentagon to improve the legal system for victims of sexual assault.

But those proposals change nothing about the way those crimes are adjudicated. The unit commanders retain the power to decide which cases to try, select juries and to overturn convictions. This is not justice.

Nevertheless, Congress, as usual, grants what the

Pentagon wants even when 26,000 men and women are sexually assaulted every year.

Wisdom on pot

The Justice Department is inching toward legalization of marijuana, a welcome development even if it is decades late.

The Feds announced that they would no longer sue to block decriminalization of pot in the 20 states and District of Columbia that have legalized it. This is a historic move by a U.S. government that once called pot "a menace to public health."

"The reform signals a long overdue acknowledgment of the costs the nation continues to pay in the indiscriminate and overzealous prosecution of its five-decade war on drugs," the New York Times editorialized.

Legalizing, taxing and regulating cannabis are in, puritanism out.

More NCAA hypocrisy

The farce of amateurism in collegiate football reached new heights recently when the Heisman Trophy quarterback Johnny Manziel of Texas A & M was suspended for *half* of a football game, a game his team was favored to win by 28 points with or without him.

Manziel's offense? He signed autographs for money, a violation of NCAA ethical rules that "besmirch the purity of student athletes." The suspension and the autograph-signing reveal for the one hundredth time the gross hypocrisy of the NCAA peddling student-athlete blarney.

The sooner the NCAA admits football is a business the better. The sooner it admits college athletes are auditioning for the pros the better. And the sooner the NCAA pays them instead of imposing sanctions for breaking "hallowed" NCAA regulations the better.

Sparks Tribune, Sept. 12, 2013

People and Places

Israelis want 'it all'

The whole civilized world is against Israel except the United States and tiny Pacific island nations of Micronesia, Nauru, Palau and the Marshall Islands.

With excellent reason. The Israelis continue to build settlements on Palestinian soil. They continue to flout international law.

Angered by the U. N. General Assembly vote to grant Palestine status as an observer state, the Israeli government will build 3,000 more housing units in areas near Jerusalem and on the West Bank. It will also withhold $100 million in tax revenues it collected from the financially strapped Palestine Authority.

As the New York Times editorialized: Israeli Prime Minister Benjamin Netanyahu's actions are "punitive and shortsighted moves that threaten to crush the Palestinian Authority and its president, Mahmoud Abbas, who has recognized Israel's right to exist."

The Times goes too far, however, when it says the actions threaten the peace process. Israel under Netanyahu does not want peace negotiations. It does not want a two-state solution. It wants it all.

"The all" was defined in a sign held aloft by a man living in Gaza: "You take my water, burn my olive trees, destroy my house, take my job, steal my land, imprison my father, kill my mother, bombard my country, starve us all, humiliate us all but I am to blame. I shot a rocket back."

The U.N. vote allows Palestine to sign treaties protecting its air space, natural gas fields off the Gaza coast and electromagnetic airwaves. And most importantly, Palestine can join the International Court of Justice and the International Court to challenge Israel's unpunished violations of international law.

Wonder of wonders

Catholic bishops voted unanimously to push for canonization of a woman who had an abortion, had a child out of wedlock, backed strikers against the Catholic Church, considered joining the Communist Party and caroused in taverns with "abandoned" young people like playwright Eugene O'Neill.

Adding to the wonder: her cause was recommended by Cardinal Timothy Dolan, conservative archbishop of New York.

His cause is Dorothy Day. It could not be worthier.

Day was an incredible woman: fiery social activist who lived like a Christian instead of merely preaching like one. She was arrested at protests for farm workers led by Cesar Chavez. She founded the Catholic Worker, radical newspaper, with Peter Maurin in 1933.

The Catholic Worker still publishes, always on the side of labor while much of the U.S. media are not. The organization has more than 200 hospitality houses. You do not have to be a Catholic to use their facilities that aid the poor: soup kitchens, rooms and clothing distribution.

In a church that has created scores of non-entities as saints, Day was a true saint.

Pope, Twitter and hope

Pope Benedict XVI has moved into the 21st century by posting messages on Twitter, a social media outlet for 1.2 billion Roman Catholics.

Is it too much to hope that now the pope will abandon his medieval stance against abortion, contraceptives and women in the priesthood?

Slavery still exists

Recent fires in Bangladeshi that killed 112 workers in sweat shops making garments for Wal-Mart make it clear that slavery still exists.

They were not "willing workers," as some defenders of capitalism insist. Workers are kept behind fences and locked 24/7 in violence-prone dorms. Companies string nets outside windows to prevent suicides.

In short, slavery in firetraps.

Sucking up to brass

William Astore, news analyst for the online TomDispatch, deplores America's "worshipful embrace of its generals."

"They've become our heroes, our sports stars and our celebrities," Astore writes. "We can't stop gushing about them."

He cites Gen. David Petraeus, even after having fallen from grace with a mistress, as being praised on CNN as "our best general since Eisenhower." Similarly, after Gen. Stanley McChrystal fell, he was called a super commander in Afghanistan.

"American culture is all too eager to raise its star generals into the pantheon of Caesars and Napoleons," Astore acidly concludes.

Justice denied

America is not the only country where politics overrides fairness. The French government proposes to raise the beer tax 160 percent.

Tax increase on wine? *Zéro, zed, rien.* France is wine country. Beer drinking is for Germans and Brits.

The French wine industry has political clout. The beer industry does not. Justice has nothing to do with politics.

Sparks Tribune, Dec. 13, 2012

Reactionary new-old pope

A letter writer to the Reno Gazette-Journal rightly characterized the new pope as "yet another old fart."

Some people might be offended by the colloquialism boldly printed by the RGJ. The writer's blunt truth, however, is undeniable.

Nor was the writer, Stuart Pardee of Gardnerville, a Catholic basher. Mr. Pardee deplored the selection of a man "who appears to have one agenda: maintain the status quo." His letter added:

"As a lifelong Catholic, I am watching firsthand the slow, steady demise of the Catholic Church because it refuses to change with the times. Sixty to 70 percent of people who attend Mass are more than 60 years old. The vast majority of priests are more than 60 years old with few studying to replace them."

Selection of a reactionary like Jorge Bergoglio of Argentina was received with joy by most Argentines. He is one of theirs. Even two UK Guardian journalists in Argentina proclaimed the election "the most radical change in the Catholic Church in more than 50 years." Not true.

Other columnists have called him "a game-changer," a terrible cliché that is also untrue.

The new Pope Francis is as medieval-minded as his predecessor, Benedict XVI.

Pope Francis will:
- War on poverty. Fine.
- Urge protection of the environment. Fine.
- Focus on the spiritual. Fine.

Other fine qualities:
- He's humble.
- He's down to earth.
- He's noted as "the slum pope."

- He's a simple guy, cooking his own dinner and living in an apartment rather than an opulent mansion.
- He sips mate, traditional Argentine herbal tea, with the folks in the baristas.
- He used public transport even as a cardinal.
- He loves soccer and the tango, Argentine passions.

But, but, but.

Francis refuses to address the church's central problem: musty doctrines. Such as:

Celibate priests, no women in the priesthood, opposition to birth control, opposition to condoms, opposition to gay marriage, opposition to adoption of children by gay couples, opposition to premarital sex and banning communion for divorced couples.

Francis opposes all those essential to bring his church into the modern era for 1.2 billion Catholics worldwide.

Liberation theology? The Jesuit Francis opposes it even though advocated by Jesuits in Latin America 50 years ago.

The aim of liberation theology was liberation from unjust economic, political and social conditions. In other words, social justice and human rights. In America, "liberation theology" has long been espoused by the socialist aims of the Catholic Worker Movement.

Detractors call it mere "Christianized Marxism." Yet there is far more Marx in Jesus than Christians will admit.

As the feisty Brazilian archbishop of Recife, Dom Héldes Câmara, said: "When I give food to the poor they call me a saint. When I ask why the poor have no food they call me a communist."

Bergogilo, as Archbishop in Buenos Aires, said of gay marriage: "It's an attempt to destroy God's plan." As Cardinal, Bergogilo said in 2010 that adoption by same-sex couples was "a war against God" and "a maneuver by the devil."

When the Argentine Supreme Court expanded access to abortions in rape cases, Cardinal Bergoglio opposed.

The absurdities are manifest. Another absurdity is his desire to restore the Latin Mass rather than the vernacular Catholics understand.

Moreover, Francis has dirty linen in his papal closet: dogged Argentine journalists suggest his complicity with the military coup that seized power in 1976 (*el golpe*). The regime kidnapped, tortured, raped, killed and caused at least 30,000 to disappear (*desaparecidos*).

Steve Wasserman of the online Reader Supported News wrote: "The atrocities reached the horror of throwing living prisoners from helicopters and airplanes into the South Atlantic."

During this dirty war the future pope was silent even when 150 priests and nuns and two bishops were killed or kidnapped.

Adolfo Pérez Esquivel, who won the Nobel Peace Prize in 1980 for defending human rights during the military horrors, said of Bergoglio: "He lacked courage to defend our fight for human rights."

As for the Argentine Catholic Church leaders in general, Professor Charles Kenney, writing for the Catholic magazine, Commonweal, declared: "They gave public recognition and support to the military dictatorship for years."

Many Argentines remain angry over the church's acknowledged failure to confront the military *golpistas*.

In any case, there is no doubting the theological reactionaryism of Francis. He refuses to baptize children of unmarried women. Argentine President Christina Kirchner proposed legalizing gay marriage and providing free contraceptives. Cardinal Bergoglio opposed.

One critic correctly compared his tone with "medieval times and the Inquisition."

Sparks Tribune, April 4, 2013

Papal resignation bodes status quo

The abdication of Pope Benedict XVI, so rare it was last done 600 years ago, offers scant hope that the Roman Catholic Church will abandon its medieval philosophy. The same fossils who chose Benedict will choose his successor.

Benedict refused to acknowledge how Catholic women actually live in the 21st century, how they repudiate church teachings.

The church is adamantly against birth control yet most Catholics worldwide practice it. Garry Wills, Catholic writer, ridicules the notion that using "a contraceptive is a mortal sin for which Catholics would go to hell if they died unrepentant."

Willis also cites the view of John Henry Newman in 1859: "History shows that the laity has been more true to the gospels than the hierarchy. For such 'heresy' the Vatican denounced him as 'he most dangerous man in England.' (The "most dangerous man" later became a British cardinal!)

The church is woefully short of priests yet will not allow women priests. It will not admit the equality of women. Sister Louise Akers, head of the Sisters of Charity, calls the Catholic Church "the last bastion of sexism."

The church insists that priests be celibate. Celibacy is unnatural. Moreover, priestly pedophilia can be attributed to the celibate priesthood. The church doesn't allowed divorced Catholics to take communion. It should. Communion is central to Catholicism.

The church prohibits the use of condoms even to prevent AIDS--a clear example of head-in-the-sand dogma. The church opposes premarital sex, a view contrary to human nature and thus practiced by few Catholics.

The introvert Benedict was mired in the past with his

books on Jesus and encyclicals on love and charity. Those things are fine for scholars and spiritual souls but dreadful leadership for the 1.2 billion Catholics in the world.

Benedict as pope constantly evaded the truth.

Jason Berry, who has written extensively about the Vatican, notes: "A long list of leaders betrayed Catholics everywhere with their pathological evasions, sending known sex offenders to treatment centers to avoid the law, then planted them in parishes and hospitals where they found new victims."

Berry describes Cardinal Roger Mahony of Los Angeles as "an egregious practitioner of the cover-up." A court ordered release of thousands of church documents revealing how Mahony mishandled sexual abusers.

The church was hammered worldwide by sexual scandal. But Benedict never disciplined bishops caught in the cover-up.

When the Irish church complained of widespread priestly sexual abuse, Benedict accused Irish Catholics of "spiritual disillusionment." Benedict denounced a group of nuns who urged liberalization of church policies.

Benedict removed an Australian bishop who suggested that priests should be allowed to marry and women allowed into the priesthood. But Benedict welcomed back an apostate priest who denied the Holocaust.

Benedict was devoid of the spirit of Vatican II and Pope John XXIII with his *aggiornamento*, the open window allowing fresh air into the church. The church needs modernization, the very revolution that Pope John desired.

Its not just a younger pope with greater energy than the frail, 85-year-old Benedict who needs a pacemaker. The church requires a younger pope in outlook, someone willing to attack "the mighty wheels of a 1,000-year-old bureaucracy," as the New York Times put it.

As for newspaper contenders, Cardinal Dolan, the archbishop of New York, is the darkest of dark horses. Even at 100 to 1 the odds are too short. The conclave has 61 Italian cardinals among the 115 eligible to vote. It is extremely unlikely it will choose an American.

Other potential papal picks come from Africa and South America. But those too are unlikely. Catholicism is declining in Europe but Italy could dominate the conclave with just 57 million Catholics. In sharp contrast, Latin America has 483 million Catholics and Africa 177 million.

The next pope? The betting by this foolish pundit is Angelo Scola.

He is 71, young enough as popes go. He is an Italian. He is archbishop of the influential see of Milan and a theologian of international acclaim. Above all, Scola fits the conservative mold of the majority of electors.

Why did Benedict quit? Italian newspapers relish Vatican scandals: banking fraud and a papal butler who leaked "juicy" gossip about Curia infighting and intrigue.

The latest: a Vatican gay network with dark tales of blackmail, theft and homosexual "infidelity." Perhaps that was one scandal too much for Benedict to cope with.

In any case, the prognosis of the College of Cardinals conclave convening next week: selection of a pope with the same musty doctrines.

Sparks Tribune, March 7, 2013

Chavez great revolutionary

America's corporate media treated the recent death of Venezuelan President Hugo Chávez with the good riddance sigh of the sudden disappearance of the black plague.

The major U.S. media, owned by six corporations, constantly misinformed and vilified him. Mark Weisbrot of the Center for Economic and Policy Research pointed out that "media reporting was effective in convincing most Americans that Venezuela was a ruinous dictatorship."

Incredibly, the Associated Press business reporter lamented that "Chávez invested Venezuela's oil wealth into social programs like state-run food markets, cash benefits for poor families, free health clinics and education." Instead, the AP reporter said, he should have built splendid buildings and glittering cities as oil-rich Middle East countries do.

The truth is otherwise. Chávez was the greatest South American since Venezuelan Simón Bolivar freed Latin America from the Spanish yoke. Chávez joins the great revolutionaries in world history like Lenin, Trotsky, Mao and Castro.

The Chávez legacy is sterling: thumbing his nose at the United States. He led Latin America nations to do likewise.

He ended U.S. dominance, "killing" the Monroe Doctrine of 1823 that warned nations to keep hands off Latin America. It was a doctrine that the United States used as a pretext for constant invasions and interventions of Latin nations.

The democratic socialism of Chavez attacked social and racial inequality. It created genuine regional integration. He inspired the rise of the Left in Latin America: Bolivia's Evo Morales, Brazil's Lula da Silva, Argentina's Cristina and Néstor Kirchner, Paraguay's Fernando Lugo and Ecuador's Rafael Correa.

André Vltchek, writing for the online Countercurrents, put it well: "Chávez knew that poor people have to be housed, fed, educated and given medical care. He knew that the wealthy world, which became rich through plunder, colonial expansion and brutality, has to stop looting and terrorizing."

No wonder the people loved him. As the UK Guardian wrote in an obituary tribute: "He appeared as an indestructible ox speaking to his people for hours in a warm, sonorous voice. His speeches contained homilies, continental and national history and quotes from Bolivar."

The people proved their love at the polls, electing him president four times.

Oliver Stone in his documentary of Chávez, despite the demonization by the American media, praised him as "benevolent, generous, tolerant and courageous."

Chávez and Fidel Castro of Cuba embraced in a common cause. The U.S. government hated Castro for daring to establish communism 90 miles from "sacred" American shores.

In 2002 President Chavez was kidnapped at gunpoint and flown to an island prison in the Caribbean sea. Pedro Carmona, a business partner of the U.S. oil companies and president of *Fedecamaras*, the nation's chamber of commerce, declared himself president of Venezuela.

As Greg Palast wrote for Truthout: the kidnapping, engineered by the villainous CIA, gave a new meaning to the term corporate takeover.

U.S. Ambassador Charles Shapiro rushed from his hilltop embassy to have his picture taken, grinning with the self-proclaimed president and the leaders of the coup d'état.

But with an armed and angry citizenry marching on the presidential palace in Caracas ready to string up the coup plotters, Carmona--the pretend president from Exxon--returned the captive to his desk within 48 hours.

Chavez had provoked the coup by clawing back some of the bloated royalties of the oil companies.

The Venezuelan leader also provoked U.S. hatred by sitting on a huge pool of oil that was "in the wrong hands." A former chief of oil intelligence for the CIA said Venezuela held a recoverable reserve of 1.36 trillion barrels, far more than oil-rich Saudi Arabia.

It's hardly surprising, then, that the right-wing hatemonger, televangelist Pat Robertson, urged the assassination of Chavez.

In any case, the failed coup did even more damage to the U.S. reputation in Latin America.

Chávez got his "revenge" in a speech at the United Nations in 2006, denouncing "the hegemonic pretensions of the American empire." Then he hurled this zinger: "The devil came here yesterday and it still smells of sulfur." (Bush had spoken from the same podium.)

As far back as 1976, long before Chavez became president, the United States in Operation Condor provided aid and resources to friendly dictators if they supported American might in South America.

Such policies, anathema to Chávez, involved privatizing national resources and selling them to foreign corporations. They also called for defunding and privatizing public programs such as education and health care.

Chávez, who idolized Bolivar, led a Bolivarian Revolution that made Latin Americans proud.

Sparks Tribune, March 21, 2013

Top Sparks cop bungler

The constable has blundered.

Supreme Court Justice Benjamin Cardozo
in 1961 (Mapp v. Ohio)

The annals of U.S. crime are full of miscarriages of justice and mistakes by police officers.

Innocent men accused of murder have been hanged. Other men have been wrongly convicted of rape and armed robbery. Still others have been wrongly sent to prison for decades.

Far less serious but aggravating to media reporters is police withholding information. Such a "shutout" happened recently after a fatal shooting spree at a middle school in Sparks, Nev.

The amateurish Sparks police chief originally withheld the name of the 12-year-old shooter in the killing of a teacher witnessed by 30 students. Only intense pressure by the media forced the cops to reveal the name as required by Nevada law.

The Reno Gazette-Journal, in an angry page one editorial, wrote: "This is unacceptable…State law is clear: the name is public information…Refusing to release the name serves no law enforcement or investigative purpose."

At first Sparks Police Chief Tom Miller declared why the name was being withheld: "We have been in contact with the parents. They are grieving and going through a very challenging, difficult time."

Compassion is fine. But it was woefully misplaced in a huge regional story. In was so big the story appeared in the New York Times, California newspapers like the San Francisco Chronicle and got extensive media coverage in Nevada.

Barry Smith, head of the Nevada Press Association, weighed in. He wrote in a RGJ column: "By attempting to hold back information investigators can do long-term harm to their communities. Gossip and speculation rush in to fill the vacuum."

Dennis Myers, news editor of the Reno News & Review, in an email to me said: "Compassion should not conceal responsibility. Government is responsible to all of us, not just to selected citizens."

Cory Farley, Sunday columnist for the RGJ, wore journalistic blinders despite 40 years in newspapering. His column has long been maundering and meandering. But the one he wrote after the Sparks murder was absurd.

He declared that the public does not need to know the boy's name. Farley added: "The family is already suffering. Why load this on them?" Answer: the public has every right to know.

Moreover, the public should know other key facts the bungling Sparks "constable" refuses to disclose. Two weeks after the shooting we still don't know what we need to know in a nation wracked by daily shooting deaths, school gun rampages and demands for stricter gun controls.

Who are the parents? How did the kid get the gun? Where was it hidden? Did the parents instruct him how to use it? Why a semi-automatic handgun?

Rumors abound if the parents are not named. Was the killer the son of a Sparks police officer? Was the shooter from a family of illegal immigrants?

Martha Bellisle, stellar reporter for the RGJ who specializes in takeouts of major community issues, says that is precisely the kind of information needed.

So a question for Chief Miller: will you ever get professional?

Dennis Myers, in an editorial in the RN&R, again brought up his context theory that he firmly believes provides perspective to the nationwide shooting carnages.

That theory holds that if a plane crashes and scores are killed context theory would say the airlines industry has an excellent safety record. True. It does. But that fact is hardly relevant to the family and friends of those killed in the crash.

The theory posits that the number of kids killed in school by guns is half of all Americans killed annually by lightning, which is to say not many. So, folks, keep in mind that schools are really safe havens. But such a theory is hardly a consolation to students, faculty and parents scarred by the Sparks shooting.

Two days after the Sparks slaying, a teacher at a Massachusetts high school was beaten to death by one of her students. But that, too, should be kept in context, folks, because as the RN&R editorial puts it: "Of all the places that children frequent, school is easily the safest."

Once again: that ridiculous theory is hardly consolation to students, teachers and parents who are in mourning.

(Since this column was written José and Liliana Reyes admitted that their son, José, was the shooter. However, they answered none of the hard questions as to how and why he had access to a gun.)

Sparks Tribune, Nov. 7, 2013

Indictment of Iron Lady horrible

The death of Margaret Thatcher makes it impossible to follow the 2,700-year-old Latin advice *de mortuis nihil nisi bonum* (speak no ill of the dead). There is nothing good to say about the woman dubbed the Iron Lady and Attila the Hen.

Indeed, "death parties" and "dancing on her grave" took place in cities like London, Belfast and Glasgow. Graffiti urged: "Rejoice! Rejoice!" and "Rot in hell, Maggie."

Another graffiti artist, punned: "Iron Lady rust in peace." Judy Garland's song from "The Wizard of Oz," "Ding Dong! The Witch Is Dead," is suddenly leading British pop charts.

This columnist refuses to rejoice over the death of anyone. But facts must be faced, reality confronted. I certainly reject the claptrap issued from the White House: "the world has lost one of the great champions of freedom and liberty."

The indictment of her as Conservative Party prime minister of Britain for 11 years is long and harsh:

• Thatcher betrayed her class. She was a grocer's daughter who served the upper classes epitomized by her husband Denis, millionaire businessman.

• She ushered in a wave of "sweeping privatizations and deregulations, legitimizing wealth and unleashing acquisitive and entrepreneurial passions," as the New York Times reported.

• She promoted Thatcherism, pushing economic freedom and demonstrating the right wing principle that "greed is good." She "propagated a faith in the redemptive power of capitalism that would dominate the world and hasten the fall of communism," the Times added.

- She smashed British unions.
- She crushed the opposition Labor Party.
- She proposed and parliament passed a regressive flat tax.
- She cut aid to the impoverished--even milk for poor kids.
- She slashed funding for the arts and academic establishments, revealing her narrow mind and provincial tastes.
- She labeled the great Nelson Mandela as a terrorist while backing South Africa's apartheid regime. She opposed Mandela's release from prison.
- She provided critical support to the odious Chilean dictator Pinochet.
- She was a steadfast friend of another brutal dictator, Suharto of Indonesia.
- She sent a British military force to retake the Falklands from Argentina in 1982, postage-stamp islands still a lingering product of colonialism. She did so against the advice of wiser heads in her cabinet. But she knew what she was doing politically, her ugly chauvinism rousing the people to re-elect her.
- She was an ally of President Reagan, her companion in reaction. They bitterly opposed communism. They declared that Cuba's Fidel Castro was exporting revolution to Nicaragua and other Latin American nations. They cut taxes for the rich.
- She granted U.S. permission to launch warplanes from British bases to bomb Libya.
- She opposed feminism and denounced homosexuality, declaring that no one had a right to be gay.
- She denounced European centralization and integration.

Such a record made her critics legion.

She thought she was "saving Britain from a working class revolution led by peace activists, the unions and Marist-Leninists," Steve Weissman writes for the online Reader Supported News. He ridiculed the notion.

Her free market policies "led to the domination of small-town life by supermarkets and other powerful corporations," another writer noted.

A former Labor Party chancellor of the exchequer called her "La Pasionaria of Privilege," callous to the plight of the have-nots.

One writer observed: "There is something creepy about this ritual of praising and proposing sainthood for political leaders like Thatcher at their deaths. It is an absurd concept."

Her hard-headed and bullying style forced the Conservative Party to drive her from office in 1990. It acted much too late. The frightful damage had been done with little hope that it will be reversed anytime soon.

Thatcher had a malignant impact on Britain. She ruined the British welfare state ushered in after World War II by Clement Attlee, the wise and prescient prime minister. His policies included the National Health Service: efficient, egalitarian and comprehensive.

The NHS was born in 1948 out of the belief that good health care should be available to all, not just the wealthy. It is free to all UK citizens.

It cannot be pointed out often enough that the United States, the richest nation in the world, still does has have national health 65 years after it was established in Britain.

Sparks Tribune, April 18, 2013

Royal birth mania absurd

The British media naturally gave the birth of a royal baby recently pages and pages of ink. But even in America the coverage was stupefying.

People magazine had a 10-page spread. Its cover line exulted: "All hail the little prince!" It also breathlessly urged subscribers to read the interview with the doctor who "delivered the prince."

The New York Times, usually a serious newspaper, gave the non-story page one news coverage and printed page-one pictures. U.S. television devoted nauseating coverage to the royal birth.

But entertainment *über alles* is the motto of the media in Britain and America. Trivia matters, not substance. A British journalism professor observed: "the media frenzy around the royal baby says everything about news-industry values."

Lionel Shriver, British novelist, noted sardonically and rightly: "The first-born of the Duchess of Cambridge (Kate Middleton) being third in line for the throne of England is of no more importance than my being third in line at my local pub."

The UK Guardian reported that the crowds outside St. Mary's Hospital in Paddington, London, "erupted in full-throated cheers" at the announcement of a royal heir: "It's a boy! It's a boy!" In the swarms of people outside Buckingham Palace, one Londoner exulted that he attended in order "to soak up history."

"Brits lavished $95 million on sparkling wine to toast the birth, $38 million on celebratory party food, $37 million on royal baby-themed toys, $86 million on commemorative memorabilia like booties and $117 million in DVDs and books, including a history of diapers that have clad royal baby bottoms," Shriver also wrote in a New York Times column.

The Royal Mint cast 2,000 lucky silver pennies, worth $45 apiece, to give to each British baby born on the same day as Prince George.

More baffling is the media mania in America. Dozens of TV cameras stationed outside St. Mary's were American, two from major TV networks. Forests of stepladders and cameras lined the hospital.

Some reporters covering the non-event camped outside the hospital for two weeks. They relieved stakeout boredom by interviewing one another, tweeting and posting notes on Facebook.

Absurdity quadrupled!

It speaks poorly of Brits and Americans to bill and coo over such insignificance. This columnist holds to the stark view of Diderot, the grand 18th century Enlightenment *philosophe.*

He constantly espoused matters of universal interest and urged international spread of ideas. The birth of Prince George is neither of universal interest nor an idea.

"Man will never be free until the last king is strangled with the entrails of the last priest," Diderot declared. Perhaps that view is too harsh in these days of powerless monarchs.

Nevertheless, royalty is a luxury Britain cannot afford with its crumbling welfare state. Neither can most countries in the world, many laden with debt and poverty, justify an obsolete monarchy.

Cromwell had it right in the 17th century: the Brits under his republican leadership abolished the monarchy. (Alas, dumber heads prevailed as the Brits later restored the royals.)

Commerce trumps nature

Yosemite National Park in California is one of most wonderful natural sites in America. Yet it has long been plagued by commercial interests. Those interests should be scrapped. Commerce mars a sacred place.

But commerce always wins. America's upside-down values prevail. Moneymaking matters, not natural wonders.

Nevertheless, the National Park Service is forging ahead with plans to remold the park's commercial heart, the seven-mile stretch along the Merced River in Yosemite Valley. It plans to restore 200 acres of meadows, reduce transportation and curb traffic and human congestion.

Above all, the Park Service plans to close rental facilities for horseback riding, biking and rafting while removing swimming pools and an ice rink.

The plan is as sensible as it is necessary. But a cretin from Congress, Rep. Tom McClintock, whose district includes Yosemite, lamented to a House committee that removing commercial facilities is meant to satisfy "the most radical fringe of the environmental Left."

The nation could use many more "radical fringes" for the environment.

Wildlife Services killings

The government's Wildlife Services is a badly named agency. Its mission is to resolve wildlife conflicts to allow people and wildlife to coexist.

Unfortunately, this has meant two million dead animals since 2000. Beavers, mountain lions, black bears, coyotes and innumerable birds are in the death toll.

As a New York Times editorial put it: "The real mission of Wildlife Services is to make life safer for livestock and games species."

Sparks Tribune, Aug. 8, 2013

105

Elder college often disappoints

Shakespeare seems to bring out the worst in reverential people: the obtuseness, the dullness and hyped-up presentation of a poet and dramatist who needs no glamorization.

Some people believe that Shakespeare can only be understood in a modern version. Thus the line from "Macbeth," "The night is long that never finds the day," is rendered in one modern version: "A new day will come at last."

The modern version is prose: flat and dull. It is a desecration. Shakespeare's line is not just poetic but perfectly expresses the long, sleepless night we insomniacs endure.

The Osher Lifelong Learning Institute (Olli), a branch of the University of Nevada, Reno, is a wonderful concept. We are never too old to study, learn and expand our horizons.

But one Shakespeare lecturer at Olli, Jim Glenn, marred the Bard with a droning, irrelevant, academic presentation.

Glenn, who has read most of the Shakespeare plays several times and seen numerous productions of them, rambled on about the genealogy of the Shakespeare family, about his wife, Anne Hathaway, and their children.

He raved about Shakespeare's studies at Stratford grammar school but not Ben Jonson's sour remark in the preface to the First Folio in 1623 that Shakespeare had "small Latin and less Greek."

The greatest poet of all time was forgotten for a discussion of trivia.

Another Olli failure is English Professor James Mardock, UNR Shakespeare specialist. He is presenting a four-part series on "Richard III." Fine. Richard is one of the great villains in all literature, his opening soliloquy magnificent.

Yet Mardock gets too technical about classical Greek views of tragedy. He uses unpronounceable words describing literary tragedy. He makes irrelevant observations about Christopher Marlowe but ignores Marlowe's "mighty line" that influenced Shakespeare.

He shows the Shakespeare text on the screen but the words are too small for some to read. He has volunteers read the non-Richard parts but some do so badly. Many readers are inaudible.

Mardock's ultimate failing: he performs rather then explains and enlightens. He cavorts, prances, runs, leaps and kneels. He has most of the elders in the auditorium laughing and applauding. But I was neither amused nor informed.

His performance reminded me of the Queen's tart observation about a Polonius speech: "More matter, with less art (manner)." ["Hamlet," act two, scene two, line 95.]

Mardock emotes Richard's lines from one spot but jumps to another spot on stage to comment on them. Frenetic and absurd. He smothers the greatness of Shakespeare with pyrotechnics.

In my view the wooing scene in "Richard III" is incredulous, perhaps the most unbelievable scene in Shakespeare. But the point is not what I--a mere lover of Shakespeare--think but what Mardock thinks. He never addresses the question.

Nor does he answer the question he poses in the Olli brochure: "The potentially most disturbing aspect of Shakespeare is his ability to bring us into his story." What's so disturbing about that? Isn't that what most authors strive for?

Olli doesn't need dull history or frenzied presentation.

It needs excitement, perhaps passion, but not dramatic turns. It needs command of the subject but not bloated presentations.

Orwell as critic

I have long admired George Orwell but my admiration grew with a New York Times review of a new book about him, "A Life in Letters." In it Orwell shared my literary tastes.

He thought F. Scott Fitzgerald overrated. I agree. Henry James "bored him unbearably." I agree.

James is often considered America's greatest novelist. I have never been able to get more than 40 or 50 pages into James' novels like "The Ambassadors," "The Wings of the Dove" and "The Golden Bowl."

In my judgment, the best James book is his novella, "The Aspern Papers," detailing the biographer's eternal search for unrevealed letters and documents.

Orwell loved James Joyce's "Ulysses" when many even today call it unreadable. I would go so far as to say "Ulysses" is the greatest novel ever written. But before you tackle that, read two excellent Joyce books, "Dubliners" and "A Portrait of the Artist as a Young Man."

'Mozart wrote that'

The gloomy Beethoven, renowned for his *sturm und drang*, did have a wry sense of humor. In 1800 he composed the Septet in E-flat in a sunny and vivacious style. Some acquaintances asked him why he did not write more compositions like it.

"Mozart wrote that," he snapped with annoyance.

Actually, Beethoven did write many non-fist-shaking compositions. One of his lightest and brightest is the marvelous "Diabelli Variations" with its little gem, "Für Élise."

Sparks Tribune, Oct. 17, 2013

Fliers urged to shun United

The best laid schemes o' mice and men / Gang aft agley.

"To a Mouse" by Robert Burns

Warning to folks flying in and out of Reno: avoid United Airlines.

This may not be possible since United has a quasi-monopoly on flights to and from Reno. (Reno is one of those smaller cities "you can't get to from here," as wags phrase it.) But be on notice: United delays and cancelled flights are constant.

One of my daughters living in Sparks puts it starkly: "We hate United Airlines. They are horrible! We have had such bad experiences with them. Other friends and family have also."

Another daughter, a flight attendant for 30 years, says: "People dislike United Airlines so much there is a Web site called 'Untied.com' (United.untied)."

My wife's family and friends have similar dreadful things to say about UA.

Her friend's husband took the scheduled mid-afternoon Reno flight to San Francisco. It was so late he had to run for his connection with a heavy bag of tools he carries as an engineer and inventor in Hong Kong. He missed the connecting overseas flight.

Subscribers to newspapers usually don't want to read about personal problems of their columnists. But the problem my wife and I had goes beyond personal woes: United made us miss our connection in San Francisco for an overseas flight to London. It could happen to you.

Our recent debacle produced the longest, most tension-riddled and most frustrating day of my life.

Our United flight from Reno was scheduled to leave at 2:30 p.m. Delay, delay, delay despite sunny skies. One excuse after another.

Then we were told our departure was set for 4:39 p.m. We never left the ground until 5:03 p.m. Nervously, we kept looking at our watches.

Finally arriving in San Francisco, we had 20 minutes to make a mad dash of one mile from the domestic terminal to the international terminal--with two security checks. We did not make it. UA failed to ask the overseas plane to wait briefly for our arrival as an attendant promised she would.

The overseas plane was booked solid for the next night. So we cancelled the London trip, our vacation shattered.

I'll skip details of the rest of the nightmare: hours getting to a hotel, finding the dining room closed when we got there. Then we learned that my wife's luggage was missing. We lost irretrievable rent money paid in advance and a second fee to change British pounds back to dollars.

We vowed never to fly United Airlines again.

Obit tells truth

De mortuis nil nisi bonum (speak no ill of the dead) is a Latin expression that is invariably observed in local newspaper obituaries. But this decorum was shattered by a paid obit recently in the Reno Gazette-Journal: a family advertisement applauded the death of the family's mother.

To my knowledge this is unprecedented. People may dislike or even hate one or both of their parents but they do not go public with such feelings.

Indeed, the usual obit paid for by the family is cloying, full of sentiments picturing the beloved deceased now sleeping "on Abraham's bosom" (Shakespeare) or maybe "walking with Jesus in heaven." But the RGJ obit was scalding in its denunciation. Excerpts:

110

- "She neglected and abused us when we were small."
- "As adults she stalked and hounded anyone we dared love."
- "Everyone she met, adult or child, felt her cruelty, vulgarity and hatred of the gentle and kind human spirit."
- "She exposed us to her evil and violent life."

So the obit writer justly celebrated her death: "We will now live in peace knowing that the nightmare has finally ended. Abusing children is unforgiveable and should not be tolerated in a humane society."

In conclusion, the obit called for "a national movement dedicated to war against child abuse."

A letter writer to the RGJ observed: "Whoever complained and thought it an awful obituary has never been abused."

Another letter said: "The agreeable response to her death notice is admirable. It is right to highlight the evil that some parents commit. I commend the bravery in writing the truth."

The real America

In yet another shooting rampage, this one recently in the Navy yard in Washington, D.C., a berserk Navy veteran killed 13 and wounded seven others.

Dr. Janis Orlowski, chief operating officer of MedStar Hospital Center, while deploring the multiple shootings, claimed that "this is not really America."

But it is. The U.S. gun culture is so deeply rooted that society will not tolerate the mildest control of and access to weapons.

Sparks Tribune, Oct. 10, 2013

PR political reporter shamed

Hugh Jackson, columnist for CityLife of Las Vegas, is the best political commentator in the state. He reveals the truth behind the truth.

Every political writer tells us that Nevada Secretary of State Ross Miller is expected to run for attorney general in 2014. Only Jackson tells us of Miller's "naked political cynicism" about voter ID.

Miller, the state's chief election officer, has repeatedly declared that voter fraud does not exist in Nevada so photo ID is unnecessary. Nevertheless, he will ask the 2013 Legislature convening next month to pass a voter ID bill.

"So why is Miller validating right-wing paranoid voter-fraud mythology even when he doesn't believe in it?" Jackson asks. "He can still run TV ads saying: 'Ross Miller fought to protect the integrity of Nevada elections by sponsoring voter ID legislation.' "

Jackson on Sen. Dean Heller of Nevada: lacks courage and conviction. During his campaign for election in 2012 Heller ran an English-version Website talking tough about "illegal" immigrants. Website in Spanish? Nary a word about "illegal" immigrants. Jackson calls it "Heller's ham-handed duplicity."

Jackson: "The war on public employees isn't about 'overpaid' civil servants and 'despicable' union 'thugs' who are 'bloating' state budgets at taxpayers' expense. It's about smothering any opposition to the ruling kleptocrats and rendering cash-based democracy even more of a farce than it usually is."

Now look at Ray Hagar, Reno Gazette-Journal political writer, columnist and unwitting public relations man for Gov. Brian ("Sunny") Sandoval:

"I say, com' on, man, cut Sunny some slack," the colloquial Hagar writes.

"In Sandoval we are dealing with a governor with a conscience. He desperately wants to do the right thing. He considers opposing views before making his decisions. It's the reason he's a political moderate.

"Sandoval, however, is still a Republican. When it comes to raising taxes, he still is against that."

Now listen to Hugh Jackson on Nevada tax policy: "Duct tape and bailing wire contraptions: raising sales taxes again, tinkering with the state payroll tax."

Jackson has pointed out many times that the sales tax is regressive. A state income tax should be progressive, based on earnings. Nevada has no state income tax. It never will until we have a courageous governor who points out the need.

Fact never addressed by Sandoval: gambling taxes in Nevada are the lowest of any state. Another fact the governor overlooks: mining has what Jackson calls a "Lilliputian tax rate."

Jackson pens "A Tale of Two Mining States": "The total mineral tax burden on Wyoming producers can be as high as 25 to 30 percent. Nevada's total burden is capped at 5 percent."

That cap is written in the state constitution. Efforts are being made to end that monstrosity but it requires another (second) approval by the Legislature and another (second) approval by the voters in 2014.

Don't hold your breath waiting for that miracle to happen.

"The mining industry is always keen to provide lawmakers with rationalizations to justify why they should not pay more taxes," Jackson writes. "But legislators should ask why the industry gets away with humiliating the state and playing Nevadans for chumps by paying such a pittance in taxes."

Nevada's "governor with a conscience" should answer that question.

But he won't. Urging even the slightest tax increase on the powerful gambling and mining industries would mar Sandoval's next political step: a run for either the U.S. House of Representatives or U.S. Senate.

Nevada's 'great' senator

The great Sen. Harry Reid of Nevada, majority leader, has urged abolition of legal prostitution in Nevada, a harmless profession but politically an easy target.

However, Reid refuses to do anything about a really tough political target: the woefully undemocratic filibuster. The filibuster requires a supermajority that constantly thwarts good legislation. It frustrates highly qualified judicial nominees.

That will not change. Reid just tinkers around the edges of the problem. As the New York Times reported: "Legislation will still be mired in murky procedural delays --just fewer of them."

Time and again Reid says he will abolish the beast. He never does. Reid is an institutionalist, traditionalist and pragmatist.

After 30 years in the Senate, Reid honors its traditions, as hoary as they are. Its rules are sacrosanct. Reform is anathema. And the Senate is far superior to the rabble in the House.

The truth about Reid: he is a gutless mediocrity.

Sparks Tribune, Jan. 24, 2013

Nation cruise disappoints

FORT LAUDERDALE, Fla.--The Nation cruise recently to the Caribbean, like many long anticipated trips, was disappointing. Some panelists were wordy, others enamored of their celebrity, others ego-tripped and several acted like standup comics rather than giving topics the seriousness they deserved.

A discussion with Nation editor Katrina Heuvel confirmed what I have long felt: America has no Left of any political significance.

The Establishment media use the phony balance of "the Right says, the Left says." But the terrible truth is that while the Right is strong, the Left does not exist except for a few voices crying in the wilderness like The Nation.

Speakers at this cruise-conference kept talking about changing American culture. But when it comes to the media, it will never change. The media are corporate and Establishment. Ownership is ever narrowing so media change is impossible.

Participants at these liberal-left conferences are overly optimistic. One cruise attendee said she was buoyed by the re-election of President Obama. The truth is that his re-election simply means more of the same.

Another woman remarked that 2012 was the most important presidential election in more than a century. Even anyone with the most casual knowledge of U.S. history cannot overlook FDR.

Nevertheless, brief biographies of the participants make it clear that so many have fought the good fight: early voting legislation, motor-voter law, teacher strikes, civil disobedience during the Vietnam War, battle to rout South African apartheid, a moving visit by an Air Force veteran to the Peace Park in Nagasaki and an activist who returned his Eagle Scout medal because the Boy Scouts are intolerant of gays and atheists.

While I dwell in the lofty ivory tower of intellectual pursuit of leftism, socialism and atheism, so many of the folks on the cruise have done far more than just theorizing. They have been active with their deeds.

The Nation gatherings for dinner each night were uneven. One evening I happily sat at the same table with Gary Younge, immediately likeable Guardian columnist, and Al Dorfman, a New Yorker and one of the few genuine leftist among the 430 Nation cruisers. Most of the diners at my table were pleasant, Nation readers, but hardly leftists.

Another criticism of these progressive meetings is that the questions from the audience so often turn into speeches. The hobbyhorses make you cry out: please creep up on your question mark.

Pro-Palestinian Medea Benjamin was the best panelist. She provided one of the highlights of the cruise, skewering the pompous Eric Alterman for his pro-Israel views.

Indeed, the Nation cruise organizers should leave Alterman home next time. At one dinner he arrogantly proclaimed that he didn't really want to be there. To prove it, he wore music plugs in his ears. Discourteous plus gall equal zero.

Stephen Cohen, Russian history specialist, proved to be another discourteous Nation star.

I asked him a serious question: is there something in the Russian psyche that demands an authoritarian state as it had under the czars and Soviets and now under President Putin? He dismissed the question with a snide reply: "Oh, you're just another Russian basher."

Hardly. Cohen, with an immense ego, is another who should not be invited again.

However, someone who ought to be invited back again and again is John Nichols. He describes the media to perfection.

"A horrible media system," he says. "The worst in the world. Dysfunctional. Even North Korea has a better media system.

"Americans believe what they see and hear on the media. They are entertained not informed by serious news. The media are led by ignorance and lies. They lead the public into unending wars. America slaughters its young people in the military."

One speaker noted the prevailing military-industrial complex but failed to add the powerful congressional influence to the complex. Members of Congress want bases, munitions depots and military facilities built in their districts or states.

Indeed, the will-o'-the-wisp fiscal cliff would vanish overnight if the military-industrial-congressional complex were greatly reduced.

During one dinner someone asked if any media outlet could be trusted. I replied confidently that he could rely on the New York Times.

But someone quickly reminded me of the Iraq war triggered by Judy Miller of the Times. And that reminded me of the pro-war corporate press and its skimpy coverage of anti-Iraq War demonstrations.

And that reminded me of the speaker who rightly ridiculed the notion of American exceptionalism. This "exceptional" nation has been waging permanent war for 70 years.

Sparks Tribune, Dec. 27, 2012

Arts and Letters

Digital information is
neither knowledge nor wisdom

DIGITAL DISCONNECT
By Robert McChesney
The New Press, 232 pages, 2013

The making of books is endless--particularly the making of bad books.

Such a bad book is this by Robert McChesney. It is especially disappointing because McChesney has been a leading media critic, writing such important works as "Rich Media, Poor Democracy" and "Corporate Media and the Threat to Democracy."

He writes about the Internet: "We are entering *terra incognita* as machines change our basic understanding of what it means to be a human." He adds these other absurdities: the Internet will "transform the world" and will "change the world beyond all recognition."

He quotes Harvard legal scholar Cass Sunstein as heralding "the development of cumulative knowledge" and "the first stages of an information revolution."

Still more McChesney claptrap: we're "building a better world" through social media. As proof he cites the social media that helped produce the Arab Spring of 2011. He does not mention the authoritarian reactions that quickly undermined those revolutions.

He fires off this tired and false cliché: "We are all journalists now." And this: "The Internet can provide the greatest journalism and public sphere ever imagined."

The Internet does not change human nature. It does not change what it means to be human. It does not "transform the world." It does not "change the world beyond all recognition."

And it certainly does not change the U.S. economic

system of gross inequality, riches for the 1 percent while so many people struggle with low wages, underemployment and 31 million below the poverty line. America will still be the same capitalist nation it was yesterday, is today and will be tomorrow.

This country will continue to elect mediocre Democratic presidents like President Obama or reactionary Republicans like Bush II. Congress will continue to house cretins who favor the status quo. And the Supreme Court will continue to hand down retrograde decisions.

McChesney talks about "living happily ever after, going to the beach with laptops, iPods, Kindles and smartphones"--all products of capitalism, all with the rapid obsolescence that capitalism demands. Nevertheless, the incorrigible McChesney hails "the glorious future of capitalism."

The book has many other problems. It is much too long. It spends vast amounts of space recounting ancient media history.

It refers to hoary authorities like Walter Lippmann and his essays written nearly 100 years ago. He dredges up Saul Alinsky, the community organizer, who insisted wrongly that "organized people can beat organized money."

He cites James Carey, guru of the J school PhDs, with such gobbledygook as this: "Alas, the press may have to rely upon a *democratic* state to create the conditions necessary for a *democratic* press to flourish and for journalists to be restored to their proper role as orchestrators of the conversation of a *democratic* society." (italics mine)

The often-cited "wisdom of the founders" is illogical and wrongheaded in two key areas: the absurd Electoral College and the horribly malapportioned and hence terribly undemocratic Senate.

The Electoral College has given the nation four presidents who lost the popular vote. The most recent was Bush II, the worst president of all.

Essayist George Scialabba notes: "Half the U.S. population sends 18 senators to Washington while the other half sends 82. California, with a population of 38 million, has two senators, the least populous states combined have 40 senators for roughly the same population as California. Senators elected by 11 percent of the population can kill proposed legislation with a filibuster."

No wonder America is a frightfully conservative nation with scant chance for progressive federal legislation such as gun controls and "dream" reform of immigration. Such as drastic state curbs on the right to abortion. Such as the Supreme Court decision Tuesday to nullify the Voting Rights Act of 1965.

McChesney tells too much about what he is going to write rather than just doing it. That's the silly academic way. Ditto with his unnecessary "academic" charts galore. Ditto with his use of clichés like "existential threat." He asks who invented the Internet? Answer: who cares?

The Internet has nothing to do with the vast ignorance of "the dumbest generation" with its appalling lack of elementary knowledge of politics, history, science and literature.

This book proves that once you are an established author you can write the veriest trash and still get your book published.

As journalism Professor Robert Jensen of the University of Texas, Austin, rightly says: "Information isn't knowledge and knowledge isn't wisdom."

Sparks Tribune, June 27, 2013

Love affair with poetry

*Poetry is when an emotion has found its thought
and the thought has found words.*

Robert Frost

The greatest Christmas gift I ever received was a
volume of poetry by Henry Wadsworth Longfellow. I was
16. The book forever hooked me on poetry. It started a
lifelong love affair with poetry's rhyme, beauty, thoughts
and wisdom.

Longfellow's "The Ladder of St. Augustine": "The
heights by great men reached and kept / Were not attained
by sudden flight, / But they, while their companions slept,
/ Were toiling upward in the night." Or these lines from "A
Psalm of Life": "Lives of great men all remind us / We can
make our lives sublime, / And, departing, leave behind us
/ Footprints on the sands of time."

I liked Longfellow's "The Children's Hour" with
"Grave Alice and Laughing Allegra" almost devouring
their professor father with kisses. And "The Village
Blacksmith" under a spreading chestnut tree with arms as
"strong as iron bands." And "The Wreck of the Hesperus,"
a schooner sailing "the wintry sea" amid falling snow
"hissing in the brine" and death "on the reef of Norman's
Woe."

There is truth in the Keats poem: "Where but to think is
to be full of sorrow." One of my favorite poems is "Dover
Beach" by Matthew Arnold. These lines: "Ah, love, let us
be true / To one another! For the world, which seems /
To lie before us like a land of dreams, / So various, so
beautiful, so new, / Hath really neither joy, nor love, nor
light, / Nor certitude, nor peace, nor help for pain."

The older I get, the more I like this insight from Yeats' "Sailing to Byzantium: "An old man is but a paltry thing, / A tattered coat upon a stick." But I cherish those defiant lines of Dylan Thomas: "Do not go gentle into that good night…rage, rage against the dying of the light."

Wilfred Owen, British soldier-poet killed in World War I, wrote these great words to anyone sickened by constant U.S. wars: "My friend you would not tell with such high zest / To children ardent for some desperate glory, / The old lie: *Dulce et decorum est / Pro patria mori*." ("It is a sweet and honorable to die for one's country.")

My all-time favorite is "Alice's Adventures in Wonderland." Lewis Carroll's nonsense fantasy never ceases to delight.

"Curiouser and curiouser," Alice cries. Encountering the tea party threesome, the March Hare, the Mad Hatter and the Sleepy Dormouse, she says: "It's the stupidest tea party I ever was at." Alice recites this enjoyable nonsense verse: "You are old Father William, the young man said… / And yet you incessantly stand on your head-- / Do you think at your age it is right?"

Carroll's sequel, "Through the Looking Glass," features Tweedledum and Tweedledee and Humpty Dumpty. And the Walrus and the Carpenter talking of many things like shoes and ships and sealing wax and asking whether pigs have wings.

My No. 2 favorite is "The Rubáiyát of Omar Khayyám" translated by Edward FitzGerald. It is a wondrous ode to hedonism, to *carpe diem*, to wine, women and song. The 12th quatrain expresses its spirit: "A book of verses underneath the bough, / A jug of wine, a loaf of bread– and thou / Beside me singing in the wilderness-- / Oh, wilderness were paradise enow!"

In between it is packed with such marvelous verses as

this: "Ah love! Could you and I with Him conspire / To grasp this sorry scheme of things entire, / Would not we shatter it to bits--and then / Remold it nearer to the heart's desire!"

It closes with an exhortation to Sákí, cupbearer to the gods: "And in your joyous errand reach the spot / Where I made One--turn down an empty glass!"

One of my favorite poems is Edwin Markham's "The Man with Hoe." It is a classic cry for socialism. Whitman is the best American poet. From "Leaves of Grass": "Walt Whitman, a cosmos, of Manhattan the son, / Turbulent, fleshy, sensual, eating, drinking and breeding." The poet says of animals: "They do not lie awake in the dark and weep for their sins, / They do not make me sick discussing their duty to God."

And this marvelous Whitman thought is dedicated to all great teachers: "I am the teacher of athletes, / He that by me spreads a wider breast than my own proves the width of my own, / He most honors my style who learns under it to destroy the teacher."

Sparks Tribune, Sept. 26, 2013

Editor skirts controversial cartoons

THE ART of CONTROVERSY
Political Cartoons and Their Enduring Power
By Victor Navasky
Alfred Knopf, 200 pages, 2013

*A caricature is putting the face of a joke on the
body of truth.*

Joseph Conrad

This book is barely worth publishing but Victor
Navasky is "somebody," editor, publisher and owner of
Nation magazine for 30 years. His writing is poor, his
reporting is poor and his judgment is poor.

A far better book is "Killed Cartoons" by David Wallis
(2007). Wallis punctures the persistent myth of the liberal
media. His target is censorship: excellent editorial cartoons
never published by the gutless Establishment media.
Wallis demonstrates that nearly all opinion editors should
be in another line of work--like clerking or accounting.

Navasky does print David Levine's great cartoon of
Henry Kissinger "Screwing the World" (1984) despite
the opposition of Nation staffers who called it a sexist
stereotype. The cartoon showed Kissinger in bed on top of
a naked woman. She had a globe instead of a head.

The cartoon was not about sex. It was about Kissinger,
secretary of state and national security adviser for President
Nixon. He was shown raping the world, his face a mixture
of ecstasy and villainy.

Tom Lehrer, songwriter and satirist, captured that
villainy: "satire died the day Kissinger was awarded the
Nobel Peace Prize" (1973).

But Navasky did not evince the same courage about the Danish cartoons satirizing Muhammad in 2005. He does not show them. (The Philadelphia Inquirer did.)

In one cartoon Muhammad is wearing a turban shaped like a bomb, the fuse lit. In another, Muhammad is standing on clouds in heaven shouting to suicide bombers: "Stop, stop! We ran out of virgins."

It is no excuse to say that nearly all American newspapers did not print them either, fearful of the furor they caused. (More than 100 people were killed and 500 injured in mêlées around the world.)

Cartoonists have shown--or tried to show--unflattering caricatures of religious leaders of all faiths, including Catholics. They are hardly sacred figures to satirists. Moreover, the vision of artists should never be censored.

Navasky offered a multiple-choice quiz as to why he did not republish the Muhammad caricatures: a) Fear of retaliation by Muslim extremists; b) Fear of booksellers wanting to avoid controversy; c) Respect for Muslim sensibilities and desire to avoid needless provocation; d) The cartoons are available on the Internet, only a Google away.

His answer: all of the above. All invalid reasons. The readers cannot judge them without seeing them. Then Navasky adds foolishly: "I have looked at the cartoons and they lack distinction." Let readers decide that.

Another glaring omission: no mention of Paul Conrad of the Los Angeles Times, the best editorial cartoonist in the country from 1964 to 1993.

Conrad, vitriolic, trenchant and mordant, was in a great tradition: Hogarth and Gillray in 18th century Britain, Frenchman Daumier and American Nast in the 19th century, Britain's Low, American Levine and Conrad's American contemporaries, Herblock, Mauldin and Marlette, in the 20th century.

Readers complained that Conrad was disrespectful of President Nixon. He was and rightly so. Great cartoonists are above presidents. They make no effort--like reporters-- to be fair and balanced.

Navasky's book is too long, marred by irrelevances, larded with clichés like "stay tuned," unnecessary "of courses" and school boy admonitions ("patience, dear reader").

He writes of the theories of cartooning like some PhD academic rather than a newspaperman: "The Neuroscience Theory," "the Image Theory" and the "Content Theory." He compounds his absurdity by sketching the "two-brain" theory, the left analytical and logical, the right creative and emotional.

Navisky notes that the National Gallery in London sells more reproductions of Leonardo's drawing, "The Virgin and Child with St. Anne and St. John the Baptist," than any other picture in its gallery. He does not show it.

After the Leonardo sold for $1.4 million, art critic John Berger wrote derisively: "It has acquired a new kind of impressiveness, not because of what it shows, but because of its market value." The price too makes the drawing worth showing.

The author proclaims himself "a free-speech absolutist" yet refuses to print the parody that caused the Rev. Jerry Falwell to file suit against Hustler magazine.

Namely: a fictional interview of intercourse "with Mom" in an outhouse ending with this comment: "I always get sloshed before I go out to the pulpit. You don't think I could lay down all that bullshit sober, do you."

The book contains one gross error: Picasso's "Guernica" is given as 1907 not the correct 1937. Navasky is even a poor proofreader.

Sparks Tribune, Oct. 3, 2013

Death of print exaggerated

Four years ago pundits were proclaiming the death of print journalism, characterizing newspapers and magazines as "dead men still walking" in the Digital Age.

I too preached that gospel of gloom and doom, even pontificating abroad by giving speeches in Athens and Oxford about anachronistic print journalism.

Yet today newspapering is a healthy business. Sunday newspapers are fat, bulging with advertising stuffers. Media giants like Comcast, News Corporation and Time Warner are glowing, surpassing Standard & Poor's average share price.

"CBS is up a whopping 40 percent," David Carr, media columnist reported in the New York Times. "The sky over traditional media is blue and it's raining green."

Yes, the print edition of Newsweek magazine died last year. U.S. News and World Report, another weekly news magazine, now focuses on college and hospital news.

But other print weeklies like The Nation, the oldest magazine in the country founded in 1865, are thriving. The reason is greatly broadened availability.

The Nation's liberal message is available in a dozen digital platforms in addition to the print version. It can be read on Zinio "newsstand": Facebook, smartphone and Kindle Fire. One of The Nation "stars" has a national television show.

Mother Jones, the investigative, reformist and progressive magazine, is still popular in print. It and the Nation are fuzzy about their circulation figures. But they serve as a counterpoint to the Establishment media that fire reporters for not hewing to corporate versions of the news.

Moreover, a lot of codgers like me prefer print editions of newspapers and magazines, cutting, saving and sending articles.

Pressure buckles Scouts

My debt to the Boy Scouts is immense. It taught me to love nature, wildlife and the environment.

It also gave me the lifelong pleasure of bird watching. To become an Eagle Scout in those days it was necessary to take bird study among the 21 required merit badges. A requirement turned into a passion.

As for homosexuality, I never heard of such a thing in my youth. Today, I know it is rank discrimination unworthy of Scouting ideals.

So it is distressing that the national Scouting board, on the verge abolishing its gay bigotry, is buckling under the pressure of traditionalists. It will put off a final decision until May. Delay probably means keeping the status quo.

Homosexuals can be excellent Scout leaders, more understanding and certainly more tolerant than hetrosexuals.

Delay also means the next step is also imperiled: abolishment of Scouting's anti-atheism bigotry. Atheists can be just as moral and ethical as kids with religious affiliations--if not more so.

Israeli bias attacked

The Israeli religious state is suddenly being confronted by talk-show host Yair Lapid. His Yesh Atid Party (Hebrew for "There is a Future") scored a stunning success in recent elections to become Israel's second largest party behind the ruling right-wingers.

Lapid rightly complained that the ultra-Orthodox are "not sharing the burden."

He wants to remove their draft exemption, integrate them into the work force and shift the balance of who pays taxes and who gets government aid.

He seeks to end the outsize influence of the ultra-

Orthodox in the public sphere. His targets are gender-segregation on buses and sidewalks and rabbinical control of marriage, divorce, conversion and adoption.

No truly democratic country would tolerate such measures, measures as strict as sharia law enforced by the Taliban and other Muslim extremists.

As one Israeli woman said of her vote for Yesh Atid: "I am so tired of the ultra-Orthodox iron grip on this country."

The ultra-Orthodox have 10 percent of the Israeli population but the power of a super-majority.

A New York Times reporter in Israel observed: "Buses have stopped displaying ads of people because portraits of women are constantly vandalized. Religious soldiers boycott military ceremonies where women sing. And women who drive on the Sabbath are often harassed."

Lapid's party platform also calls for same-sex marriage and an end to inequality in family law.

His is a fight for the soul of Israel.

Benighted land

A few brave souls in this benighted land of 325 million Americans defy attempts to shove religion down their throats. Such a one is Amadee Martella, 18, of Spokane, Wash.

"Ever since I heard my middle school science teacher say the hand of God was responsible for separating the continents, I have become a freethinker, promoting the separation of church and state in public schools," she said.

To solidify her point, Amadee is majoring in evolutionary biology at the University of Colorado, Boulder.

Sparks Tribune, Feb. 7, 2013

Last Supper shows Leonardo genius

LEONARDO AND 'THE LAST SUPPER'
By Ross King
Walker, 275 pages, 2012

"The Last Supper" by Leonardo da Vinci is the most famous painting in the world. It has been copied in many ways, among them oil on canvas, paint on wood and molded terra cotta and marble. It stars in wax museums and hangs in countless homes.

"Over the centuries it has been depicted in illuminated manuscripts, carved in ivory and on stone and woven into tapestries," author John King writes. "It appeared at the Chartres cathedral in the middle of the 12th century on magnificent stained glass."

The painting adorns the Dominican refectory, Santa Maria delle Grazie in Milan, a marvelous work 15 feet high and 29 feet long.

Leonardo seldom finished any project because he was distracted by thinking about, observing and studying mathematics, geometry, astronomy and architecture. And war implements: designs for wheeled-gun carriages, machine guns and tanks.

He was constantly taking notes.

"Perhaps no one in history ever drew as much as Leonardo or felt such a compelling need to record on paper everything he saw," King writes. "Whenever he went for a walk he tucked into his belt a sketchbook to record the faces, manners, clothes and bodily movements of people he saw."

But Leonardo not only finished "The Last Supper," he worked a miracle as he always wanted to do on his projects. He revealed in this work his "universal genius" that Bernard Berenson spoke of in "The Painters of the Italian Renaissance."

Like all writers, King needed a demanding editor. The book is filled with clichés, repetitions and tedious passages. It's at least 75 pages too long, giving unnecessary history and too much detail about wars of the era. Sometimes the book is nicely illustrated in color, at other times the sketches by Leonardo are faint and unclear.

But worst of all, King suffers from the ailment of so many biographers: suppositions rather than facts. His book is riddled with these typical phrases: "may have," "almost certainly," "must have," "probably," "presumably," "no doubt" and "seems to have."

Some critics argue that the painting is now 80 percent by restorers and just 20 percent by Leonardo. There is much truth in that. But the brilliance of Leonardo is evident in "The Last Supper."

Vasari, biographer of the great Renaissance artists, marveled at Leonardo's "beautiful and detailed drawings, unrivalled for the perfection of their finish."

Here's King on "The Last Supper":

• "Besides commanding the center of Leonardo's painting, Christ is spatially isolated from the apostles all of whom are bunched together as they touch their neighbors or lean across them. Leonardo further highlighted Christ by placing him against a window that opens onto a landscape of clear sky and bluish contours--in effect a halo."

• Leonardo ignored "the religious hocus-pocus of the gospels and simply used their narrative to offer a scientific and psychological exploration of human behavior worthy of Freud."

• He was fascinated by the expressive possibilities of the hand, facial expressions and gestures so they abound in 'The Last Supper.' "

• Leonardo finished the painting in 1498 after "working erratically" on it from his scaffold in the refectory, "sometimes painting furiously from dawn to dusk without stopping for food or drink at other times studying the mural for hours without touching his brushes."

• " 'The Last Supper' " combined intensity of color with subtlety of tone, storms of movement with delicate grace of line, symbolic beauty with vivid narrative and distinctive characterization. Above all, it possessed life-like details--from the expressive faces of the apostles to the plates of food and pleats of the tablecloth."

Christ's face is the most expressive, sad-eyed and sad-faced, reflecting the passage in Matthew 26:21: "Verily I say unto you, that one of you shall betray me."

Leonardo's refectory tableau captures the drama and excitement of the gospels. Judas is a dramatic figure in the painting. Leonardo shows him clutching a money bag, a symbol of his betrayal of Christ.

"Judas' mantle is blue in shadow and green where, as he reaches for the bread with his left hand, the light from Jesus' window catches and illuminates the scene," King notes. "Leonardo was fascinated by what light and shade could do to color, revealing character by exposure to light."

Floods damaged "The Last Supper." Napoleon's generals stabled their horses under the masterpiece and their soldiers pelted the pictured apostles with pieces of brick.

Worst of all, an RAF bomber blew off the refectory roof in 1943. Miraculously, the painting survived. Leonardo admirers are richer for it.

Sparks Tribune, March 14, 2013

Lautrec ' steals' exhibition

SAN FRANCISCO— Exhibits of French Impressionists and Post-Impressionists often reveal works I have never seen or "noticed" before despite decades of going to art exhibitions in America and Europe.

So it is with the William Paley collection of 60 paintings showing here through Dec. 30 at the de Young museum in Golden Gate Park. The exhibit contains several gems.

The best is Mme. Lili Grenier, an oil portrait by Toulouse-Lautrec painted in 1888.

Kenneth Baker, San Francisco Chronicle art critic, says the portrait has "astounding descriptive flair."

Indeed it does. Mme. Grenier is imperious, self-satisfied. Her lower lip is curled downward, barely concealing contempt. Her hair is red. Lautrec adored redheads.

She is slouched in a chair. Colorful brush strokes dot her kimono. She's knitting, reminding you of the Dickens character, Madame Defarge, in "A Tale of Two Cities."

The Lautrec portrait, just 18" x 21 ¾," is magnificent.

Mme. Grenier, a Belle Époque beauty, modeled for Lautrec. According to Lautrec biographer Gilles Néret, she was "his best and most perceptive woman friend." Lautrec admired her great warmth that went along with her attractiveness.

Paley, co-founder of CBS, bequeathed his collection to the New York Museum of Modern Art where the portrait usually resides. Paley's treasure includes a who's who of Impression and Post-Impressionist painters like Francis Bacon, Bonnard, Cezanne, Degas, Derain, Gauguin, Lautrec, Matisse, Picasso, Renoir and Vuillard.

As with so many works of art and literature, individual taste is everything. I detest the facial distortions of Bacon but many viewers find them excellent. I think Gauguin, admired by many art lovers, is vastly overrated. Cezanne is a great artist but his still lifes have no appeal to me.

I dislike Picasso's cubism but his 1906 painting at the de Young, "Nude With Joined Hands," from the rose period, is winning.

Also winning is Picasso's "Boy Leading a Horse" (1905-1906). The boy is nude, his right fist clenched. No reins are visible but the viewer easily "sees" him leading the horse. The canvas is a gray pale blue.

Matisse I find uneven. But I like his "The Musketeer" in the Paley collection. The oil, painted in 1903, shows the gallant swashbuckler leaning on a sword and wearing knee-high boots.

Here's a game for you: when next you visit an art exhibition ask yourself which one picture would you take home if it were given to you. At some art exhibits I find none. The Paley show has one: Mme. Grenier.

Poor Richard

"Richard III" is one of my favorite Shakespeare plays, ranking close behind "Hamlet," "King Lear," "Macbeth" and "Henry IV, part one" (Falstaff).

But the "Richard III" recently presented here in the Live Oak Theater in Berkeley was so bad I walked out at the intermission. Amateurish and boring. Women shrieked instead of acted.

The play was set in the 1920s. In some productions modern dress works if the adaptation is true to the words of Shakespeare.

But this production was terribly anachronistic. A Victrola played in several scenes. Richard's henchmen, appearing twice in the background wearing military uniforms, shot and killed royal successors to the throne.

Alas, this was not the "Richard III" I love. The deformed

Richard, since he cannot "prove a lover," is determined "to prove a villain."

When you have seen the best on stage, in movies, on VCRs and videos you should never go to third-rate productions.

Siege of Troy

Berkeley Repertory Theatre staged a one-man tour de force by Henry Woronicz as the poet retelling the Trojan War.

The play, "An Iliad," written by Lisa Peterson and Denis O'Hare, was accompanied by bassist Brian Ellington "hidden" in the balcony. He played soft notes or thunderous chords depending on Woronicz's passion or subdued moments.

The play, without an intermission, needed one. But even with an intermission, the play was too long even at one hour and 40 minutes. We had too much of Achilles battling Hector.

The best part of the play: the poet's five-minute recital of wars of history from Alexander the Great and Genghis Khan, through multiple crusades, including the Children's Crusade. And still more wars: the terrible, senseless litany of wars up through Korea, Vietnam, Iraq and Afghanistan.

At that point the play should have ended. But, no, it trailed off into 20 minutes of anti-climax.

Theater-going is always a gamble. Sometimes viewers are disappointed. "An Iliad" has its moments but ultimately failed.

Sparks Tribune, Dec. 6, 2012

Bad book from academia

CAN JOURNALISM SURVIVE?
An inside look at American newsrooms
By David M. Ryfe
Polity, 198 pages, 2012

Dr. David Ryfe, journalism professor at the University of Nevada, Reno, has written an academic journalism book. This means a bad book.

It is a terrible model for journalism students: poorly written, dull and twice as long as necessary. It badly needed a rigorous editor.

Dr. Ryfe belabors what has long been obvious to anyone who has followed the woes of the newspaper business for almost a decade.

Circulation declining, ad revenues down, online revenues disappointing, print newspapers folded, print newspaper editions being reduced and staffs slashed. More and more people are getting their news and opinions online.

Dr. Ryfe repeats an enormous amount of newspaper history that is not only dull but has nothing to do with the survival of newspapers today. The book is packed with stale "news" and tedious facts. So much here is "so what?"

Dr. Ryfe says the book was written for students as "a spur to their creativity and ingenuity."

Vain hope. The book is a hard, hard slog. Only a reviewer would have the persistence to stick it out to the end.

An early warning arises in the book blurbs: "lively ethnographic detail" and "extensive ethnographic field work." Ethnographic?

A sterner warning comes in the introduction: 28 pages of scholarly garbage. The reader is informed of study after study: "e.g., Barabási, 2002; Ferguson, 2002; Schnettler, 2009."

Clichés abound: the unnecessary "of course" as in "of course, Kovach and Rosenstiel are wrong." "Framed" as in "as I have framed the issue." "Template" as in "the template required stories to be shorter." "Doubled down." And reverse sexism: "If you ask a journalist what a reporter is *she* will reply...." Men are also reporters. "Famously" as in "famously discovered" or "famously" said.

And this: "Culture derives from the Latin root *cultis* meaning 'to makes things grow' as in 'to cultivate.' " And this: "A theory of situated learning." And this: "organizing work in granular form." And this: "Newspapers copied the success of other newspapers--a process social scientists refer to as 'isomorphism.' " And this: "adopting the new practice is not normative...or epistemological...but ontological."

And, yes, the beloved academic charts and graphs to show the "node, hub and bridge" of things. Or, as the book calls it, a "cyclic-entropic developmental model."

Spare us the "journalistic" academician and the academic pedant.

Dr. Ryfe says public opinion on the death penalty "became stable in the early 1980s and remained much the same the rest of the decade." That opinion? The author doesn't say. A good editor would have written a query demanding an answer.

Too often Dr. Ryfe tells readers what he is *going* to say rather than just saying it. He gives credence to the thoroughly discredited citizen journalists carrying laptops and hence "changing" journalism. He cites the "two-step flow theory of communication" promulgated in 1955. (1955!)

The names of newspapers he visited, studied and coded stories by their reporters are fictitious. Names of reporters are fictitious when quoted or given attribution. Journalism should be fact, not fiction.

Research and scholarship are necessary in universities. But in journalism they are good only for promotion to full professor.

Dr. Ryfe omits the real problem with the nation's press: it is Establishment whether in the Reno Gazette-Journal or the New York Times. The viewpoint in columns and editorials is mostly conservative.

So many columnists are poor writers. They are dull like Nicholas Kristol and Thomas Friedman of the New York Times. And they nearly all are typical of the corporate media.

Take Times columnists Maureen Dowd and Gail Collins. They are school-girlish. If that sounds sexist I remind you of the late, great Molly Ivins. Her sparkling columns told the unvarnished truth. Times columnist Bill Keller is a blowhard. Paul Krugman of the Times is the best of a dreary lot but often writes the same column using different wording.

TV news is superficial. Sunday pundit shows are woefully unbalanced. In 2011 the has-been Sen. John McCain, an Arizona conservative, appeared 10 times. Appearances of Sen. Bernie Sanders, a liberal-leftist from Vermont? Zero.

Newspaper editorial and opinion pages are devoid of passion, barren of anything that makes readers delighted or angry. Newspapers lack that individual voice to lift them above mediocrity.

What newspapers sorely need are writers like H.L. Mencken who, in the words of biographer William Manchester, "opposed everything respectable, mocked everything sacred and inveighed against everything popular opinion supported."

Sparks Tribune, Nov. 29, 2012

Wanted: stern editors

Today's sermon is on editing, an oft-told tale but one that needs constant retelling. Namely: all writers need a demanding editor no matter how long they have been professionals.

I have been writing for 65 years, beginning with high school and college sports. Yet still today I see my columns in print and wish I had changed a word, rephrased a sentence or deleted a line.

I seek what Flaubert did: *le mot juste*, the exact word.

What would a vigorous editor say of the following beginning to a recent campus newspaper story about the inauguration of President Johnson?

"This Friday will mark the continuation of a tradition the University of Nevada has upheld for decades. From the university's first president, LeRoy D. Brown, in 1887, through Milton Glick in 2011, the University of Nevada, has always held high standards for its leaders, and its (sic) about to add one more to its repertoire."

A stern editor would see that that "lead" is jammed and repetitious, know that repertoire is the wrong word, the paragraph has unnecessary commas and contains a grammatical error.

But the biggest problem: it's PR. It reads like--and probably was--a handout from the UNR communications department.

The editor of the campus paper, the Sagebrush, doesn't know anything about editing. Everything written is just shoved into the newspaper. But the Sagebrush is published by students. You can't hold them to tough editing standards.

The Reno Gazette-Journal has no such excuse. It ran this headline about the event: "UNR tradition endures at Johnson inauguration."

This paragraph followed: Johnson promised to "pursue

a course rooted in the decency…that has characterized this institution."

Fine words but PR words. Here's the harsh truth:

• The Regents, after months of squabbling, fired President Max Milam without a hearing, causing a faculty uproar. Historian Jim Hulse called it one the worst episodes in UNR annals with "North versus South and an agriculture dean who insisted on running his own fiefdom contrary to university policy."

• President Minard Stout was autocratic. He fired five faculty "troublemakers," two esteemed biology researchers and three high-caliber English professors.

• President Glick canned two campus stalwarts for daring to blow the whistle on UNR wrongdoings.

• President Joe Crowley, an insider, was anointed by Regent Bob Cashell despite better qualified applicants.

• President John Lilley left in disgrace, despised by faculty and staff.

• One Regent demanded that acting President Johnson be hired as president rather than any of the more qualified outsiders.

Journalism requires the five W's: who, what, when, where and why. It should add a T for truth.

I edit even while reading books. I recently read that public opinion on the death penalty "became stable in the early 1980s and remained much the same the rest of the decade."

That opinion? The author didn't say. A good editor would have written a query demanding an answer.

Grades, grades, grades

I often found teaching a trial in recent years. This is an audio-visual age. Students want to be entertained, not enlightened. They demand power point, not old-fashioned lecture and discussion.

143

But far worse: too many students today think only of grades. Not ideas, not thoughts, not critical thinking, not insights--just grades.

Such an attitude renders education meaningless, undermining the whole point of a college degree.

One student earned a C in my media law class last spring although she never scored better than C+ in any test, term paper or book review. She never brought the text to class. But she did bring an iPad, punching away during class.

Nevertheless, she still appealed, demanding a B.

The journalism academic chair, Dr. David Ryfe, ruled for her--a gross injustice. He chose her self-evaluation rather than my 30 years of student evaluations.

The issue is one of standards. A university demands excellence. Calling mediocrity good debases that standard.

Her baseless appeal and Dr. Ryfe's decision angered me. But far more important is the fact that my classes are wasted on such students. They offer so much more than the subject matter.

I tried to inculcate a love of literature. Sometimes I'd quote a few lines of poetry. I urged an interest in history and politics.

I would say, for example, that Thomas Paine was one of the greatest men who ever lived and tell why. My hope was that someone, some day would read Paine's works out of intellectual curiosity.

For receptive students the class offered what critic Edmund Wilson called "animated conversation, gaiety and an uninhibited exchange of ideas."

Sparks Tribune, Nov. 1, 2012

Abolish journalism schools

Emory College in Atlanta is closing its journalism program. All other journalism programs in the country should do likewise.

"It's not our job as a liberal arts college to train people to be professional journalists," Emory arts & science dean Robin Forman said.

He's right. The greatest problem with J schools: they are hag-ridden with PhDs, scholars and theorists. They teach "coding," "aggregated content" and social media networking. They create "apps" and computer games.

A PhD journalism professor just wrote a book about the survival of newspapers. He discussed "ethnographic field work," "ontological bedrock," "epistemology," "isomorphism," "situated learning," "constitutive rule," "high modern phase of journalism" and "the theory of journalism."

To PhDs, newspaper reporting and writing are afterthoughts. But this is hardly new. It has just gotten worse.

The Association for Education in Journalism at its annual convention in 1965 had divisions of theory and methodology, public relations, radio-TV, magazine and international relations. It had no newspaper division.

A year earlier at the AEJ convention a professor said he *believed* the Freedom of Information bill had been passed recently by the Senate. It had been enacted by Congress and signed by the president two months earlier. Apparently reading a newspaper is unacademic.

Dickens in the "Pickwick Papers" satirized such academic folderol with the Pickwickians accepting a paper on "Speculations on the Source of the Hampstead Ponds with some Observations on the Theory of the Tittlebats."

A communications conference in Honolulu this

year increased contempt for academic research. Dreary papers were read on such arcane topics as "Nietzsche and the Grateful Dead: Transformative and Collective Improvisation."

Academe magazine (May-June 2011) cited the anti-intellectualism prevailing in J schools. It noted that academic disciplines like media history and public affairs reporting have been eliminated, replaced by sports writing, sports public relations and sports marketing, ecommerce, web design and animation.

Blame it on the PhDs. Communicology has ruined J schools.

When Joseph Pulitzer founded the journalism school at Columbia he declared: "It will be the object of the school to make better journalists, who will make better newspapers, which will better serve the public."

Fine aim. But Columbia succumbed to the chi-squares (PhD's). A devastating article in the New Republic in 1993 quoted a Columbia professor as constantly asking students what was "the null hypothesis" of stories they wrote. One exasperated student finally blurted out: "My null hypothesis is that the Columbia Journalism School is all bullshit!"

People who want to be journalists certainly need a college education, just not a journalism degree. They need a much wider range of knowledge. They need literature, prose and poetry. They need knowledge of movies, history, art and classical music and opera. They need to be abreast of national and world news and politics.

Most journalism professors are mediocre. They have no passion except for the views of the reigning Establishment and corporate media.

Advertising? It's a craft, a skill--but it is the art of selling which should not be taught in J schools. Public relations? It is spinmeistering. It is flackery which has no place in J schools.

Defenders of journalism education say that at least their ethics courses are essential. Nonsense. They are meaningless if their future bosses in print and broadcast sometimes don't have ethics.

A profound question almost never asked in J schools: is it ethical to make enormous profit at the expense of good newspapering? Is it ethical to slash staffs, offer less by reducing reporting and columnists, abandon investigative reporting, do little government reporting and close bureaus?

Moreover, J school professors are softies, giving out far too many good grades to average students. A study of the 2008-2009 school year at the University of Nevada, Reno J school showed 76 percent of the students got A's or B's (33 percent A's and 43 percent B's).

This is not just grade inflation. It is contrary to what I found in five decades of teaching.

J schools have another problem: corporate backing. Don Reynolds is an example of a bad journalistic name attached to a J school.

Good newspapering never occurred to him. Money-making was all that mattered. The only name worse for a J school would be William Randolph Hearst, sensationalist and inventor of news. But the Reynolds foundation and endowment give millions to the Reynolds School of Journalism at the University of Nevada, Reno.

Still, no problem is worse than the learned PhD professors: they know nothing about writing and can't teach it. They make a mockery of journalism education.

Sparks Tribune, Nov. 15, 2012

Scientology credibility boundless

INSIDE SCIENTOLOGY
By Janet Reitman
Houghton Mifflin Harcourt, 369 pages, 2011

I had a colleague teaching journalism at Wayne State University in Detroit decades ago with a brilliant son who became a Scientologist. He and his wife were horrified.

With good reason. Scientology is a fraud. It has been exposed in articles and books for 60 years. Yet still today it has called the fastest growing belief in America. The credibility of people is as astounding as it is boundless.

Author Janet Reitman tells how Ron Hubbard transformed a self-help group into a spiritual corporation. His greatest coup: getting a billion dollar tax exemption as a religion from the gullible IRS.

The fact is that Scientology is a business, not a religion, with marketing, advertising and PR. Along the way Hubbard got movie star Tom Cruise to serve as a front man.

Hubbard ruled for 25 years with charisma, fear, intimidation and hucksterism.

Scientology has been sued many times, once this year for duping members into donating $420,000 for non-existent disaster relief and a building campaign. The money was pocketed by cult leaders and fattened cult coffers.

Steve Sebelius reviewed a book about Scientology for CityLife of Las Vegas in March. The book, "Going Clear: Scientology, Hollywood & the Prison of Belief," by Lawrence Wright, tells how believers are mistreated, punished for petty statements and "thought crimes." Punishments included confinement in horrid conditions, hard labor for little or no pay and beatings.

An E-meter audits practitioners. A description alone

tells you how fraudulent the cult is--and how little it has to do with religion. The E-meter (electropsychometer) measures galvanized skin response. The sect treats it as a religious artifact recording the static field around the body.

Jeff Sharlet, in his exposé review in the San Francisco Chronicle, called Hubbard "a relentless teller of tale tales" who lied about his abysmal Navy record and boasted of his "uncanny powers." [Claims of magical powers emanated from charlatans like Rasputin (sanctity through sex) and Mesmer (energy and spiritual transference between animate and inanimate objects).]

A review by Michael Kinsley in the New York Times was just as devastating. Kinsley, editor at large of the New Republic, is no radical and the Times is hardly Marxist. He noted how Hubbard babbled about Venus and Mars like the science fiction writer he was.

Kinsley says naïve doesn't begin to describe the likes of Cruise and his ilk: "Their credulousness and sense of entitlement have allowed Hollywood actors, writers and directors to think they were helping themselves and the world by hanging around Scientologists, taking upper-level Scientology courses and gossiping about 'suppressive persons' (bad guys)."

Reitman's view is equally shattering. Hubbard's claims are "totally outlandish." She observes:

• "Traditional religious bedrocks--worship, God, love, compassion and faith--are absent from Scientologist precepts."

• "Scientology charges members for every service, book and course offered, promises greater spiritual enlightenment with every dollar spent. People don't 'believe' in Scientology, they buy into it."

• "The buying and selling of self-betterment, an American concept, has never been more in demand than it is today."

• "The church owns great quantities of real estate all over the world for which it paid cash."

• "Hubbard preached that Scientology was the only way out of the maze of the human condition."

He claimed millions of members in 165 countries in church, missions and outreach groups. As with any mesmerizing leader, huge Hubbard portraits adorned Scientology functions.

His book, "Dianetics," was published in 1950. It's heft: 452 pages. It's opening: absurdity: "The creation of 'Dianetics' is a milestone for man comparable to his discovery of fire and superior to the inventions of the wheel and the arch."

It may have been the most derided book in history: little science, lack of empirical evidence for assertions, claims of embryo memory and long discussions of life in the womb.

Isaac Asimov, who knows as much about science fiction and as he does about Shakespeare, called the book gibberish.

Further proof of the speciousness of the book was Hubbard's supposed revelation of "the exact anatomy of the human mind." His next step: Scientology allows the practitioners "to discover the anatomy of the human soul."

Hubbard, who died in 1986, was a quack. His Scientology, the "study of truths," has no truths.

Criticism of the Reitman book is plentiful: no photos; too many annoying abbreviations like "he'd," "she'd," "they'd" and "who'd"; a book much too long by 100 pages; and marred by a weak ending rather than the powerful sum-up indictment her book warrants.

Nevertheless, she draws a damning portrait of Hubbard and Scientology.

Sparks Tribune, May 9, 2013

Clichés and clutter
mar the art of writing

Clutter is the disease of American writing. We are a society strangling in unnecessary words, circular constructions, pompous frills and meaningless jargon.

William Zinsser "On Writing Well"

Monkey see, monkey do.

Writers and headline editors are like that. They see words and phrases in print and republish them so often they become clichés.

We have President Obama's "signature" health care legislation, a basketball team's "signature" moment, a "signature" achievement, a "signature" remark, a cyclist's "signature" poker face, a photographer's "signature" photo and an ultra-orthodox rabbi's "signature" black hat. Almost anything is iconic or an icon: "iconic day camp" and "porn icon."

People and organizations no longer oppose. They "push back." The cliché "shock and awe" now extends to soccer teams. "Gut check." "Pro-active." "Riff." "Push comes to shove." "Bottom line." "Avatar." "Horrific." "Quirky." "Cutting edge." "Mojo." Grandmothers with an "attitude." "Toxic." "Arguably" as in "sanitation workers are arguably invisible." Clichés all.

More: "We are all Trayvons now" (untrue cliché)... "we are all secularists now" (untrue cliché) ..."never looked back"..."stunk out the joint"..."elephant in the room"..."800-pound gorilla"..."Faustian bargain"... "dystopian"...Orwellian, Hegelian and Hobbesian (life is "nasty, brutish and short") ..."buzz" or "buzzword"... "child's play"... "not rocket science"... "metrics"... "algorithm"... "business model."

Articles are sprinkled with the unnecessary "of course," a vastly overused and usually useless expression. As in: "The most famous book, of course, is." Or: "I'm referring, of course, to J.M. Barrie." Everything is "famously" said. "She famously coined the phrase." A soccer team "*famously* wears red and black and a cyclist has "famous" sideburns.

A San Francisco Chronicle writer refers to "Oscar Wilde's infamous play 'Salome.' " It was infamous only in the warped minds of British censors.

"Existential" is a tiresome cliché but sounds intellectual. "Life's great mysteries seem existential." "Existential" dread. "Trope" is fancier than theme. The cliché "meme" sounds more learned than an idea, behavior or cultural usage. How many readers understand when writers use words like genome?

More clichés: "learning curve," "sweet spot," "slam dunk," "bent out of shape," "pitching a fit" and "rolling your eyeballs" (or "raising your eyebrows"). "We're shocked, shocked." "One great leap for..." (fill in the blank). Obama's "legacy" is on the line or his "legacy" legislation. Football and basketball coaches are "legendary." Teams are "on a roll." Golfers no longer sink putts. They "drain" them.

"Systemic." "A-list." "Fingers crossed." Families get "closure." "Looks like a million dollars." "No more Mr. Nice Guy." "Push the right buttons." "Go with the flow." "Been there, done that." "Win-win situation." "The long and the short of it." "She got *in touch* with her kinky side," "*channeling* Coltrane" (or whomever) and "*think* Harrison Ford, gunslinger in Cairo."

Other clichés: "at the end of the day," "back in the day," "eye-opening," "eye-popping," "back story," "boggles the mind" and "spike" (for rise). They "nailed it," "speak truth to power" and "transparency." Stores and abortion clinics

152

are "shuttered," never closed. "I have your back," "tweak" the tax plan, going "viral," "thrown under the bus," "go for it," "*pantheon*" of visionary film directors" "synergy," "growing like kudzu" and "say what?"

Still others: every social critic is a "public intellectual." "Game over." "Gaming the system." "End game"... "Rubber-stamped." And that meaningless phrase: "The world as we know it." "End Medicare *as we know it*." "Redefining the memoire *as we know it*." Many newspapers still cannot say died in obituaries, using euphemisms "passed away" or "passed on."

And still more clichés: "under the radar," "light at the end of the tunnel," "ramp up," "firestorm," "stay tuned," "unintended consequences," "fast track," "beef up," "self-fulfilling prophecy," "fuzzy math" and "raising the bar." Movie critics are fond of calling films *noir or noirish*. Unbelievably, the Reno Gazette-Journal recently referred in an editorial to "tossing her hat in the ring."

Did I forget "train wreck" as in "teacher-testing train wreck"? Or "gaining traction"? Or "over the top," "draw a line in the sand" and "man up"? Or, "enabler," "edgy," "tempest in a teapot," "holy grail," "crown jewel" and "deconstruct" as in "deconstructing Obama's speech"? "Wall-to-wall TV coverage," "cobble together," "boys of summer," "make my day," "end of story" and "it makes your head spin"? "Take with a grain of salt," and "who knew?"

And "time to *move on*," "get over it," "template," "boots on the ground" and "faux" as in "faux patriotism"? And "cut to the chase," narrative as in "austerity narrative," "bells and whistles," give a "shout out" (praise), "smack-down," "eye candy," "uptick" (increase), "circle the wagons," "no brainer," "cottage industry," "tip of the iceberg," "beef up," "free gift" and "leave no stone unturned"?

And, "think outside the box" and "silver bullet" or "magic bullet." And "muse" (usually a woman but sometimes a man), "poster boy" or "poster child" and "rubber hits the road"? "That's the way the cookie crumbles," "minimalist," "jaw-dropping" and "mind-blowing"? And "dialectic," "holistic," "blowback," "sum-zero," "wiggle room," "tie the knot," "sea change," "ah-ha moment," "my bad," "bodice ripper," "the right call" and a "no-no"? "Bring it on" and on car anachronisms *think* hideaway headlights?

And: "take it to the next level," "double down," "call out" (criticize) and "usual suspects." "Game changer," "outlier," "take no prisoners." Clichés all. "Wake-up call," "in play," "gravitas," "retro" and "bet the farm." And: "The ball is in Egypt's court," "the Magna Carta of voter suppression," "turn the state on its head" or "stand on its head," "physically *challenged*," political "odd couple" and paintings "fetch" $5.6 million at auction. Clichés all.

More clichés: "hot-button issue" and "count 'em" as in "150 dancers--count 'em." And: "gold standard," "no-brainer" and "ratcheting up." And: "circle the wagons," "throw the book at," "step up to the plate," "cottage industry" and more women are going to college, *"thank you very much,"* "good news, bad news," "I've seen this movie (scenario) before" and "rollout" (start) as in "Obamacare insurance marketing rollout."

And: "radioactive," "painted into a corner" and "deer in the headlights." And: "cheer to the echo," "light bulb goes on," "world class," "political football," "go back to the drawing board" and "she weighs 106 pounds *soaking wet.*" And: "last hurrah," "bring it on," "awesome," "on the bubble" (or housing bubble and artificial bubble), "wiggle room" and "say what?"

And: "it sucks," "too much on his plate," "he has his back" and "the emperor has no clothes." The San Francisco

Giants are toast and the wolves in Yosemite are toast too. Every alleged scandal is a gate suffix as in "bundlegate." "Motherhood and apple pie." Endless clichés. "Hard act to follow," author's *"victory lap,"* "watering hole," *"visionary"* filmmaker *et al* and "who knew?"

Just *one* movie review in the New York Times had *five* cliché words and expressions. Paul Krugman, Times columnist and rare liberal economist, is a master of clichés. One of his columns had four: "dropping like flies," "bites the dust," "over the top" and "that man in the White House."

Unbelievably, some writers still use "hats off to." Also: "well" as in: "Mormons practice a really, *well*, religious religion"…"Er" as in: "Can you diagram this Sarah Palin word-salad, *er,* sentence?" Clichés all. "Ahem" as in "a layman, *ahem*, more Catholic than the pope." (double cliché)… "Um" as in "an attempt at, *um*, humor." And the schoolboy aside: "Are you ready for this?" More clichés: Everything is "framed" or "book-ended." We "seal the deal" and "hit the wall."

I defy you to go through a day's reading of newspapers, magazines and online stories without spotting a cliché.

This sentence has two clichés: "a *dysfunctional* Congress is a *new normal*." We get the learned sounding "cognitive dissonance." Presumably everyone knows what that means but I doubt it. Merriam-Webster's Collegiate Dictionary defines it as "psychological conflict resulting from incongruous beliefs and attitudes held simultaneously." Better to use that rather than write incomprehensibly.

Ditto "intuitive" (feeling of truth without reasoning) and "counter-intuitive." Write it understandably. Ditto "counter-productive." "Reductive." "Productive dissonance." Write it plain. Avoid sesquipedalian (long and windy) words and phrases.

Some writers, trying to show that they are not sexist, write: "If you don't hook the reader from the start you may not catch her at all." Reverse sexism. Men are also readers. Make it plural *readers* with the object *them*.

Here's another clichéd usage: "Welcome to the Digital Age." Here's a word that no good writer ever uses: utilized. Columnist Russell Baker described it as "a fat, greasy, dripping word." Lunch is "washed down" with wine. A cliché and a misnomer. Wine is to be savored, not merely to "wash down" food. And: "you're *so* yesterday." "The wait is 269 years and *counting*."

Rather in "*rather* twisted idea" wastes a word. So does "a *somewhat* depleted team." So does "a *pretty* reasonable plan." So does "*back* in 2008." So does: "will the wide receiver actually, *you know,* speak?"

Too many people write "at about 7 a.m." No need for two prepositions. Too many write "for better or worse," a meaningless, contradictory cliché. How can something be both? It's similar to writing: "it may or may not." "Kanaan *may* win Indy car triple crown"? He may not. "Two *could* run for office." They also could not. "More or less." It can't be both. A columnist will begin, "As you may have heard." Readers may not have heard.

Never use the "latter and the former." The phrase forces readers to read the sentence again to find out who's who. The first paragraph will say that the soccer player is not for sale. Several graphs later the writer quotes someone saying the same thing. What does neo-liberal mean? Neo-conservative?

Another fault: "famous Excel error." I don't recall what that was. People write CPI on first reference. Better to write it this way: "Consumer Price Index (CPI)." Readers need reminders. (The well known FBI or CIA need not be spelled out on first reference.)

Mannerisms hobble writing: "It is the drop that nobody seems able to, *well*, drop." Or, interjections like "oops." Or, "hypocrisy, thy name is *(duh!)* Washington." Or writing, "*Raise your hand if you think.*" Or, "all these sort of, you know." Or, "she's allegoric to grass--sort of." Or, *whoa* in sentences. Or, injecting in stories, "*no kidding.*" "You--*yes, you*--can vote." He accepted--*gasp!*--illegal goods. "They prefer to be called champions, *thank you.*" Wasted, meaningless words. Or: "She orders every page redone in shades of, yes, you guessed it (pink)."

Another writing cliché: "Ms. del Lago, meet Ava Gardner." Another: "Operation Iraqi filmmaker" or any other kind of operation. And cluttered sentences: "She believed in Dom Pérignon for the makeup chair, in gifted, turbulent men (husbands Mickey Rooney, Artie Shaw and Frank Sinatra, yes, but also Robert Mitchum, Howard Hughes and a few too many bullfighters.")

Or, sophomoric constructions: "Oh, joy, we're all rich again! Or not." Or writing, "he was arrested for--*you guessed it*--sexual assault." Or, "He even missed--*gasp*--overheads." A French president is described as "uncharismatic and unauthoritative (*read* unpresidential)." Read is a mannerism.

More wasted words: "I *kind of* wanted." "It was kind of out of my control." "I don't consider it, *like*, a streak." "To be fair." Just say it fairly. "To be clear." Just say it clearly. "Full disclosure." If it needs disclosure just disclose it. "To repeat." Just repeat. ("That's right: we said *off-the-job rights.*") "One *small* problem: he couldn't have been the killer." That's hardly a small problem.

And teenager talk: " I was drinking Fantas *like* twice a day. And I was thinking *like*." "And I'm *going* (thinking)." And the grating "have a nice day" purred by strangers as they step off an elevator. A friend had a marvelous bumper sticker: "I'll have any damn kind of day I please!"

And how many times have you read a variation of silliness like this: "make the world anew" or "help us change the world"? Or, "transform the world"? Or, "change the country"? Or, "game changing"? "19ᵗʰ Amendment changed U.S. politics forever"? Or, "change history"? Or, "end of history"? Or, meaningless "post-modern"? Or, "this column will change your life"? Or, "this confusing world"? Or, steamboat-cruise hyperbole: "A journey like no other."

Or, "thanks to bank collapses"? That's hardly something to be thankful for. "The show's title naturally calls to mind." Leave out naturally.

Or, this book-jacket blurb: "the media revolution that will begin the world again." Or, a firm making a "marketing and cultural revolution." Revolution is too fraught with meaning to be used for selling. Apocalypse and apocalyptic are too prevalent. And that barbarism, "weather-wise" and other "wises." After every disaster like the Boston Marathon bombing we get nonsense columns like this: "Time for sports to help us heal again."

All writers have a style. I prefer the Hemingway style rather than the Faulkner style. But the tastes, wishes and preferences of writers differ. For example, some writers--men and women--want to be perceived as leathery so they use barnyard language like "fuck up," "bullshit" and "bird shit." On a movie: "A piece of shit." Such words are not arguments.

However, this can be carried to extremes of Puritanism. Will Durst, San Francisco columnist, writes: "One reason no one gives a rat's behind about America's Cup." Any writer with an ear for words would write "rat's ass." Similarly, it is not a barnyard epithet to write of a "piss-poor" leader. It's colorful slang usage. Bum-bussed is coy usage for the better expression: ass-kissing.

I know highly intelligent people who cannot utter a single sentence without lacing it with obscenities. I also know intellectuals who cannot speak a single sentence without using two "you knows."

In all this difficult business of writing, even for professionals of long-standing, let's not forget that editors, like Homer, can either nod or not know any better. Take this ungrammatical headline in a recent New York Times: "Series of explosions rocks." It does not take a grammarian to know the verb should be rock for a plural subject.

Online writers are weak on grammar. They often don't know the difference between "to lay off" (verb) and "layoff" (noun). The committee held *its* meeting not their. He *emigrated* from Australia, not immigrated from Australia. He is an immigrant from Australia.

He is "14-years-old"? No hyphens. But as a compound modifier: a 14-year-old boy. Editors sometimes confuse the there/their/they're and to/too and it's/its. The congressman brings home "the proverbial bacon"? There is no such proverb.

"*Like* I said." I should be *as* I said. Some write that "the lions *lay* down with the lambs" (lie). They call the Supreme Court majority radical when the proper word is reactionary. Even professional journalists write: "The Bay Area media winds up. *Wind* up since media are plural. Or writers insist on using the euphemistic football "*program*" instead of writing about the football *team*.

Newspaper copyeditors let these redundancies get into print: "lone gunman," "primary election," "currently writing a book," "small village," "3 a.m. in the morning," "a small handful," "young teenager" and "I interviewed him in person." Or, they let writers get away with turning nouns into verbs: "he is *tasked* with," "pandas *birthed* twins," "she *referenced* the information," "Cheney *primarying* in Wyoming" and "Giants *gifted* a win."

Newspapers print: "America is *quietly* selling arms to Mideast allies." How else, with a blare of trumpets? Many copyeditors don't know that the question mark goes outside the quote in: "War of northern aggression"? And here's a pet peeve: "A TED call." What's that?

Nothing was more depressing as a journalism teacher than the inability of students to write well. Their writing was murky, repetitious, ungrammatical and irrelevant. Perhaps they were unfortunate enough to suffer from insufferable academic writing.

But I am being unkind to students. The art of writing is difficult enough for long-time professionals let alone for young people.

Many people use clichés in conversion. Expressions like "that's the living end" and "long in the tooth." They are easily understood, often used unthinkingly. But writers should, *well, ahem,* shun clichés *like the plague.*

Written for Reno News and Review, summer 2013

Gift book of Longfellow launched
my love affair with poetry

Poetry is the rhythmical creation of beauty in words.

Poe

Poetry is when an emotion has found its thought and the thought has found words.

Frost

The greatest Christmas gift I ever received was an illustrated volume of poetry by Henry Wadsworth Longfellow. I got it from a friend of my mother in 1947. I was just 16. The book forever hooked me on poetry.

Longfellow is not a profound poet in the sense that Dante, Goethe and Shakespeare are. But that Longfellow book started a lifelong love affair with poetry's rhyme, beauty, thoughts and wisdom.

Longfellow's "The Ladder of St. Augustine": "The heights by great men reached and kept / Were not attained by sudden flight, / But they, while their companions slept, / Were toiling upward in the night." Inspiring, hopeful lines to a dreamy youth.

Or these lines from "A Psalm of Life": "Lives of great men all remind us / We can make our lives sublime, / And, departing, leave behind us / Footprints on the sands of time." Not immortal poetry but magnificent to a boy.

I remember the truth in Longfellow's "My Lost Youth": " 'A boy's will is the winds will, / And the thoughts of youth are long, long thoughts.' " I liked Longfellow's "The Children's Hour" with "Grave Alice and Laughing Allegra" almost devouring their professor father with kisses. And "The Village Blacksmith" under a spreading chestnut tree with arms as "strong as iron bands." And

161

"The Wreck of the Hesperus," a schooner sailing "the wintry sea" amid falling snow "hissing in the brine" and death "on the reef of Norman's Woe."

Taste and judgment in literary matters, as in all things, are individual. My taste may not be yours. Indeed, some of the poems I think highly of are sometimes not anthologized.

British poetry

Over the years "my taste" seized on some of the following poems.

Marlowe's "Dr. Faustus" with these wonderful lines: "Was this the face that launched a thousand ships, / And burned the topless towers of Ilium? / Sweet Helen, make me immortal with a kiss. (He kisses her) / Her lips suck forth my soul: see where it flies! / Come, Helen, come, give me my soul again."

I like the absurdity in John Donne's "Song": "Go, and catch a falling star, / Get with child a mandrake root." I like the twin Milton poems, "L'Allegro" and "Il Penseroso." "L'Allegro": "Hence loathed melancholy / Of Cerberus and blackest midnight born, / In Stygian cave forlorn / 'Mongst horrid shapes, and shrieks, and sights unholy." "Il Penseroso": "Hence vain deluding joys, / The brood of folly without father bred."

Milton's "Paradise Lost," a religious epic, is not one of my favorite poems. But I love the fact that the rebellious devil gets its best line: "Better to reign in hell than to serve in heaven." I like the thought of Pope's "Essay on Man": "Worth makes the man and want of it the fellow; / The rest is all but leather or prunella."

I like Thomas Gray's "Elegy Written in a Country Churchyard": "The curfew tolls the knell of parting day, / The lowing herd wind slowly o'er the lea." And then these sad lines from "The Epitaph": "Here rests his head upon the lap of earth / A youth to fortune and to fame unknown: / Fair science frowned not on his humble birth, / And melancholy marked him for her own."

More from Gray's "Elegy": "the madding crowd's ignoble strife," "some heart once pregnant with celestial fire" and "full many a flower is born to blush unseen." And this stanza: "The boast of heraldry, the pomp of power / And all that beauty, all that wealth ever gave, / Awaits alike the inevitable hour, / The paths of glory lead but to the grave."

I had to memorize "The Epitaph" in a high school English class. Most kids hated the assignment but I loved it. My teacher, Miss Koehler, solidified my passion for literature. She was one of those teachers we remember as long as we live.

The older I get, the more I like this insight from Yeats' "Sailing to Byzantium: "An old man is but a paltry thing, / A tattered coat upon a stick." And speaking of intimations of mortality, I cherish those defiant lines of Dylan Thomas: "Do not go gentle into that good night / Old age should burn and rave at close of day; / Rage, rage against the dying of the light."

William Blake is often too religious for my taste but his opening stanza of "Auguries of Innocence" is worth memorizing: "To see a world in a grain of sand, / And a heaven in a wild flower, / Hold infinity in the palm of your hand / And eternity in an hour. / A robin redbreast in a cage, / Puts all heaven in a rage."

The Robert Burns poem, "To a Mouse," is well known. His "To a Louse" should be better known because of this great passage: "O wad some power the giftie gie us / To see oursels as ithers see us!"

As an environmentalist I cherish these lines from Wordsworth: "The world is too much with us: late and

163

soon, / Getting and spending, we lay waste our powers: / Little we see in nature that is ours; / We have given our hearts away, a sordid boon!"

I love the opening lines of Keats' "Ode to a Nightingale": "My heart aches, and a drowsy numbness pains / My sense, as though of hemlock I had drunk." There is truth in the Keats poem: "Where but to think is to be full of sorrow." And what stout soul can resist Tennyson's line in "Ulysses": "To strive, to seek, to find and not to yield"?

One of my very favorite poems is "Dover Beach" by Matthew Arnold. Its "moon-blanched land," its "grating roar of pebbles" and its "melancholy, long, withdrawing roar." Then these lines: "Ah, love, let us be true / To one another! For the world, which seems / To lie before us like a land of dreams, / So various, so beautiful, so new, / Hath really neither joy, nor love, nor light, / Nor certitude, nor peace, nor help for pain."

Walter Scott was a novelist but will probably be remembered only for this line of poetry: "Oh what a tangled web we weave when first we practice to deceive!"

Wilfred Owen, British soldier-poet killed in World War I, wrote these great words to anyone sickened by constant U.S. wars: "My friend you would not tell with such high zest / To children ardent for some desperate glory, / The old lie: Dulce et decorum est / Pro patria mori." ("It is a sweet and honorable to die for one's country.") Robert Southey makes a more subtle anti-war point in the last stanza of "The Battle of Blenheim": Little Peterkin was asked what was the good of the battle. "Why, that I cannot tell," said he, / "But 'twas a famous victory."

George Moore was an Irish novelist, playwright and poet (1852-1933). Some of his poems were erotic. One is "The Triumph of the Flesh": "I am filled with carnivorous lust: like a tiger / I crouch and I feed on my beautiful prey:

/ There is nought in the monstrous world of Astarte / So fair as thy body." (Astarte is the Babylonian goddess of love.)

Nor should we forget the nonsense verse of Edward Lear providing smiles of pleasure: "The Owl and the Pussy-cat went to sea / In a beautiful pea green boat, / They took some honey, and plenty of money, / Wrapped up in a five pound note."

The Reno News & Review is hardly the prudish "family newspaper" published by the Establishment press. Yet it is unlikely to print limericks because to be any good most limericks must be "indecent."

Here's one, written by "anonymous," printed in many variations but all printable: "A fairy once in Khartoum / Invited a lesbian up to his room / But they spent the whole night / In a helluva fight as to who / Should do what to whom."

Here's an example of the "other" kind: "There was a young plumber of Leigh / Who was plumbing a girl by the sea. / She said, 'Stop your plumbing, / There's somebody coming!' / Said the plumber, still plumbing, 'It's me.' "

British novelist Arnold Bennett calls "plumbing" the best limerick ever written. Perhaps. But with more than 1,300 in print there is room for disagreement. Two recommended books are out of print but possibly available at Amazon: "The Limerick," edited by G. Legman, Portland House, and "Poetica Erotica," edited by T.R. Smith, Crown Publisher.

My all-time favorite is "Alice's Adventures in Wonderland" written by Lewis Carroll with illustrations by John Tenniel. The nonsense fantasy of "Alice" never ceases to delight. I reread it every year or so--and always with pleasure.

"What is the use of a book without pictures or conversations?" Alice asks with wisdom beyond her years.

"Curiouser and curiouser," Alice cries. Encountering the tea party threesome, the March Hare, the Mad Hatter and the Sleepy Dormouse, she says: "It's the stupidest tea party I ever was at in all my life." Alice recites this enjoyable nonsense verse: "You are old Father William, the young man said… / And yet you incessantly stand on your head-- / Do you think at your age it is right?"

Carroll's sequel, "Through the Looking Glass," features Tweedledum and Tweedledee and Humpty Dumpty. And the Walrus and the Carpenter talking of many things like shoes and ships and sealing wax and asking whether pigs have wings. And the nonsense verse of all nonsense verses is "The Jabberwocky": " 'Twas brillig and the slithy toves / Did gyre and gimble in the wabe; / All mimsy were the borogoves, / And the nome raths outgrabe."

My No. 2 favorite is "The Rubáiyát of Omar Khayyám" translated freely by Edward FitzGerald. It is a wondrous ode to hedonism, to *carpe diem*, to wine, women and song.

The 12th quatrain expresses its spirit: "A book of verses underneath the bough, / A jug of wine, a loaf of bread–and thou / Beside me singing in the wilderness-- / Oh, wilderness were paradise enow!" It closes with an exhortation to Sákí, cupbearer to the gods: "And in your joyous errand reach the spot / Where I made One--turn down an empty glass!"

In between it is packed with such marvelous verses as this: "Ah love! Could you and I with Him conspire / To grasp this sorry scheme of things entire, / Would not we shatter it to bits--and then / Remold it nearer to the heart's desire!"

Oscar Wilde's "The Ballad of Reading Gaol" shows his serious side as opposed to the wit, epigrammatist and esthete. One memorable stanza is printed on the Jacob Epstein sphinx sculpture at Wilde's grave in Père Lachaise cemetery in Paris. "And alien tears will fill for him / Pity's long-broken urn, / For his mourners will be outcast men, / And outcasts always mourn."

Émile Zola, the great French writer, once complained that English was a barbarous language. Wilde, in perhaps the greatest putdown in literary history, sighed and said: "Yes, I have been condemned to speak the language of Shakespeare." It was also the perceptive Wilde who wrote in "De Profundis": "Shakespeare is the most purely human of all great artists."

H.L Mencken started to compile a book of quotations but quit when he realized he had a preponderance of quotes by Shakespeare. Mencken was right. How can you resist the marvelous poetry of "In such a night" in "The Merchant of Venice"? Or Romeo's tribute to womanhood: "But soft, what light through yonder window breaks? / It is the east and Juliet is the sun."

And the sonnets, so many wonderful ones. One of my favorites is XXXV: "No more be grieved at that which thou hast done: / Roses have thorns, and silver fountains mud; / Clouds and eclipses stain both moon and sun, / And loathsome canker lives in sweetest bud."

Read Harold Bloom and Isaac Asimov for more erudite and profound insights about Shakespeare. My views are those of an amateur in the sense of an admirer, devotee and lover rather than a professional critic.

To me, the most poetic of Shakespeare's plays is "Macbeth." "Macbeth says his way of life "Is fallen into the sere, the yellow leaf; / And that which should accompany old age, / As honour, love, obedience, troops of friends, / I must not look to have but in their stead / Curses not loud but deep, mouth honour, breath, / Which the poor heart would fain deny and dare not."

Then: "Tomorrow, and tomorrow, and tomorrow / Creeps in this petty pace from day to day / To the last syllable of recorded time; / And all our yesterdays have lighted fools / The way to dusty death. Out, out, brief candle! / Life's but a walking shadow, a poor player, / That struts and frets his hour upon the stage / And then is heard no more. It is a tale / Told by an idiot, full of sound and fury, / Signifying nothing."

"Hamlet" is the most cerebral although it too has some memorable poetry. "King Lear" is the bleakest. In Lear the cruel Regan says of the blinded Gloucester: "let him smell his way to Dover." And earlier Gloucester remarks: "As flies to wanton boys are we to the gods; / They kill us for their sport."

"Richard the III" contains perhaps the most lovable villain in literature. Richard says: "I am determined to prove a villain." He succeeds admirably.

American poetry

I'm not wild about Frost as many American poetry lovers are. But I do like "The Death of the Hired Man." It reminds us to be kind to someone who "comes home to die," to abandon our narrow-mindedness, to be more generous about the foibles of people. Nor do I fancy Emily Dickinson, a poet beloved by English teachers. Dickinson is "nice." (I know: terribly patronizing.)

To me, Whitman is the best American poet. Look at his "Leaves of Grass": "Walt Whitman, a kosmos, of Manhattan the son, / Turbulent, fleshy, sensual, eating, drinking and breeding."

The poet says of animals: "They do not sweat and whine about their condition, / They do not lie awake in the dark and weep for their sins, / They do not make me sick discussing their duty to God." Like Shakespeare, Whitman knows bird lore: "Where the mockingbird sounds his delicious gurgles, cackles, screams, weeps."

And this marvelous Whitman thought should be

dedicated to all great teachers: "I am the teacher of athletes, / He that by me spreads a wider breast than my own proves the width of my own, / He most honors my style who learns under it to destroy the teacher."

One of my favorites is Edwin Markham's "The Man with Hoe." It is a classic cry for socialism. It starts: "Bowed by the weight of centuries he leans / Upon his hoe and gazes on the ground / The emptiness of ages in his face… / Stolid and stunned, a brother to the ox… / Through this dread shape humanity betrayed, / Plundered, profaned and disinherited / Cries protest to the powers that made the world."

I'm mostly indifferent to T.S. Eliot with his fancy words without meaning. To me his best poem is "The Love Song of J. Alfred Prufrock" with its amusing nonsense. Does he dare to eat a peach? He measures out his life with coffee spoons. "I grow old…I grow old… / I shall wear the bottoms of my trousers rolled." And grant Eliot that great line in "The Hollow Men": "This is the way the world ends / Not with a bang but a whimper."

Edna St. Vincent Millay is a fine poet. Her "Recuerdo" (Spanish for memory) is a 16-line poem about a couple spending a happy night on a ferry. But, sensitive to the feelings of others, the couple shares their happiness with a babushka. Here's the ending:

"We were very tired, we were very merry, / We had gone back and forth all night on the ferry. / We hailed, 'Good morrow, mother!' to a shawl-covered head… / And she wept, 'God bless you!' for the apples and pears, / And we gave her all our money but our subway fares."

I love Poe's "The Raven" with its hammering, repetitious sounds: "While I nodded, nearly napping, suddenly there came a tapping, / As of someone gently rapping, rapping at my chamber door." Then this wonderful stanza:

"Open here I flung the shutter, when, with many a flirt and flutter, / In there stepped a stately raven of the saintly days of yore. / Not the least obeisance made he, not a minute stopped or stayed he, / But with mien of lord or lady perched above my chamber door-- / Perched upon a bust of Pallas just above my chamber door."

My granddaughter Kami Moloney, who goes to Reed High in Sparks, recalls memorizing a famous poem and reciting it for a Mendive middle school class project. "I chose 'The Raven' because I enjoyed the words that Poe used and the story they described," she said.

Recently she and I were talking to the library director of the Nevada Historical Society. For no apparent reason, we began quoting to her lines from "The Raven." The librarian was delighted by the *extempore* recital. We were even more delighted.

People without a similar love for poetry are poorer.

Written for Reno News and Review, Summer 2013

Civil disobedience extols conscience above law

Sometimes one must take a position that is neither safe, nor politic, nor popular but he must take it because conscience tells him it is right.

"A Testament of Hope," writings and speeches of Martin Luther King

Henry David Thoreau, little known and unsung, is one of the greatest American heroes, far greater than soldiers cited for bravery or generals who triumph on the battlefield.

Thoreau is worthy of being "canonized" for two works alone: "Civil Disobedience" and "A Plea for Captain John Brown." Both are in the wonderful American tradition of dissent. As Thoreau noted in Walden: "Public opinion is a weak tyrant compared with our own private opinion." Or, in "Civil Disobedience": "There is little virtue in the action of masses of men."

In "Civil Disobedience" Thoreau asked, "Must the citizen ever for a moment resign his conscience to the legislator?" His answer was thunderous: no!

"I think we should be men first and subjects afterward," he wrote. "It is not desirable to cultivate respect for the law so much as for the right. Law never made men a whit more just. And by means of their respect for it even the well-disposed are daily made the agents of injustice."

Thoreau added: If the law requires you to be an agent of injustice "then I say break the law." That's why he defended Brown with moral outrage and indignation.

Brown broke the law in 1859 with an attack on the federal arsenal at Harper's Ferry, hoping for an uprising of 4 million slaves. He thus obeyed a higher command: his conscience. Slavery was wrong. It must be abolished at once.

"I would rather see the statue of Captain Brown at the Massachusetts state house than that of any other man I know," Thoreau declared. "We talk about representative government but what a monster of a government it is where the noblest faculties of the mind and of the whole heart are not represented."

Namely: John Brown.

Thoreau, calling him "a sublime spectacle" and "an angel of light," asked: "When were the good and brave ever in a majority?" He agreed with Brown: "a man has a perfect right to interfere by force with the slaveholder." Brown said his "rifles and revolvers were employed in a righteous cause," a cause expressing his "sympathy with the oppressed and wronged."

Brown presciently concluded that Civil War was the only way "the Negro question" would be resolved. He knew too the truth in Thoreau's essay "Life Without Principle": "What is it to be free from King George and continue the slaves of King Prejudice?"

Even the Great Liberator, William Lloyd Garrison, initially thought that Brown was going too far to take action to free the slaves. Garrison thought words were enough. As he wrote, "I do not wish to think or speak or write with moderation. I am in earnest. I will not equivocate. I will not retreat a single inch. AND I WILL BE HEARD."

Brown knew better. Abolishment of slavery must come about through deeds, not words.

Birmingham rebellion

Martin Luther King, as a student at Morehouse College in Atlanta, was greatly impressed by "Civil Disobedience." He came to the same conclusion as Thoreau. Words were not enough. He realized you had to break the law even if it meant going to jail in order to smash the chains of segregation.

The rebellion began with Rosa Parks in 1955. A bus driver in Montgomery, Ala., ordered Parks to give up her seat to a white passenger. She refused. She said she was tired of being treated as an unequal human being.

The bus driver had her arrested under Alabama law. Her pastor, Martin Luther King, was so incensed he launched the Montgomery bus boycott. The civil rights movement had begun.

Inspired by Gandhi's non-violent satyagraha ("soul force"), King in 1960 lauded Southern black college students for their sit-ins at lunch counters while facing "hoodlums, police guns, tear gas and jail sentences."

In 1963 he wrote the moving "A Letter From a Birmingham Jail." He excoriated the "vicious lynch mobs and hate–filled policemen who curse, kick, brutalize and even kill." He denounced white and colored signs in the South. He deplored the indignity of being called "nigger" or "boy." He noted "a degenerating sense of 'nobodyness.'"

King's words resounded with cries for freedom. Freedom rides. Freedom trains. Freedom marches. He wanted to free blacks from racism and whites from the burden of racism.

King reminded Americans that by denying freedom to blacks they had "left the house of their great heritage and strayed into a far country of segregation and discrimination. In the midst of all your material wealth you prove spiritually and morally poverty-stricken, unable to speak to the conscience of the world."

King gave his best-known speech, "I Have a Dream," during the March on Washington in 1963. It was the greatest demonstration for freedom in the nation's history.

"We have come to our nation's capital to cash a check," King said. "When the architects of our republic wrote the magnificent words of the Constitution and the Declaration of Independence, they were signing a promissory note to

173

which every American was to fall heir. This note was a promise that all men, black and white, would be guaranteed the unalienable rights of life, liberty and the pursuit of happiness."

Then those marvelous, repetitive, rolling cadences:

"I have a dream that one day this nation will rise up and live out the true meaning of its creed: 'We hold these truths to be self-evident: that all men are created equal.' I have a dream that one day on the red hills of Georgia the sons of former slaves and the sons of former slave owners will be able to sit down together at the table of brotherhood. I have a dream that one day down in Alabama, with its vicious racists, little black boys and black girls will be able to join hands with little white boys and girls as sisters and brothers."

Most Americans came to accept King's dream. But many could not accept King as a social critic, declaring that he should stick to civil rights. Not so. His social criticism was also powerful.

He rightly indicted America's Vietnam War. He flayed the nation's "spiritual death" in spending more on the military than on "programs of social uplift." He denounced capitalism. He deplored the gap between the rich and the poor.

King's social criticism is an old, old American tradition.

Mark Twain, outraged by U.S. suppression of the Filipino revolt, declared that America ought to paint the white stripes on its flag black and replace the stars with the pirate skull and cross-bones. Suffragette Susan B. Anthony led demonstrations for women's right to vote, going to jail for voting illegally in 1872.

Margaret Sanger advocated birth control early in the 20th century, opening the nation's first birth control clinic. She was driven to advocate birth control because her mother endured 18 pregnancies in 22 years. Bob La

Follette, Wisconsin senator, deplored the invasion of Nicaragua in 1927. He described it as "harsh, bullying, an unjustifiable action setting Central and South American countries against us."

In 1946 socialist Norman Thomas lamented the fact that 3,200 Americans were jailed for the "crime" of conscientious objection. Pullman car unionist Philip Randolph scored Jim Crow as an "unmitigated evil." He pointed out the absurdity of a segregated army. Justice Douglas decried the manufactured Red Scare in the 1950s, spawning character assassination and rampant fear.

In our day, President Obama's treatment of whistleblower Pfc. Bradley Manning is unconscionable. For nearly three years Manning has been held in a military prison, subject to torture and other inhumane treatment. Locked up naked in a cage. It's one more blot on the American escutcheon.

Manning's crime? Supplying a trove of documents to the world, documents that are no threat to national security but a gross embarrassment to America. The government charge of "aiding the enemy" is patently absurd. He merely wanted to provoke "worldwide discussion, debate and reform." The world rewarded him with much discussion and debate. Reform, alas, is beyond the capacity of the U.S. government.

"His repressive treatment is one of the disgraces of Obama's first term," Ed Pilkington of the UK Guardian declared. "Obama not only defended Manning's treatment but also as commander in-chief of court-martial judges improperly decreed his guilt when he asserted that he broke the law."

Manning is a classic whistleblower. The public appreciates his leak of astonishing examples of systematic U.S. subversion of worldwide democracy, including killings and atrocities. Governments do not appreciate such candor.

David Coombs, lawyer defending Manning at the military trial in Fort Meade, Maryland, pointed out that his client disclosed the documents, not as "a reckless act to undermine national security," but as an "act of conscience designed to expose government misdeeds and defend the public's right to know."

Governments abroad react the same way with another great leaker, Julian Assange. The British consider him an "enemy of the state." Assange released hundreds of thousands of diplomatic cables showing U.S. war crimes, collusion with death squads in Iraq, lies of U.S. allies, and spying on U.N. officials.

U.S. politicians and right-wingers want Assange designated a terrorist. An absurdity. But nothing is absurd to a U.S. government determined to conceal embarrassment.

First Amendment rights of Manning and Assange are being denied. As so often in hypocritical America, free speech has its limits. The government tried to block publication of the Pentagon Papers on the grounds of violating national security. Fortunately, even a conservative Supreme Court saw through that charade in its 1973 decision.

Professor Howard Zinn supported civil rights while teaching at Spelman College in Atlanta. He was fired by Boston University for supporting striking union workers on his campus. He gave a defense of civil disobedience while attacking the Vietnam War, declaring that it was essential to break unjust laws in order to achieve fundamental rights.

Boxer Muhammad Ali refused induction into the Army in 1967 during the Vietnam War. He declared, "I ain't got no quarrel with them Vietcong."

Most Americans were outraged. So-called liberal columnist Tom Wicker denounced Ali as "painfully warped in spirit." Sports columnist Red Smith "smelled" the "stench emanating from the induction center." The FBI tailed and wiretapped Ali. The World Boxing Association stripped Ali of his heavyweight title.

States refused to let him fight. In Nevada, Gov. Paul Laxalt denied an Ali-Floyd Patterson fight with a phony rationale: It would be a mismatch. The Johnson administration stripped Ali of his passport to prevent him from fighting overseas.

At the trial for "refusal to submit to induction," a jury deliberated 20 minutes before sending him to prison for five years. In 1967, his peak as a great champion, Ali was barred from the ring.

"It was a marvelous demonstration of the value of civil disobedience [in publicizing injustice] and an inspiration to our generation — particularly to those soldiers and sailors who opposed the Vietnam War," said Dennis Myers, news editor of the Reno News & Review. Myers was one of those soldiers.

Glorious court dissents

Despite the many terrible decisions by the Supreme Court throughout history, some great dissents have illustrated what it means to be an American.

It does not mean wearing flag pins, flying flags on pickup trucks or draping houses with huge American flags. It means dissents as in In re Yamashita (1946).

In that case the court upheld the hanging of a Japanese general ordered by a military commission, declaring that the findings of a military panel were unreviewable. Justice Frank Murphy dissented because the general was denied a fair trial.

"No exception is made to those who are accused of war crimes or those who possess the status of an enemy belligerent. Indeed, such an exception would be contrary to the philosophy of human rights that makes the Constitution the great living document that it is.

"The immutable rights of the individual belong not alone to the members of those nations that excel on the battlefield or that subscribe to democratic ideology. They belong to every person in the world, victor or vanquished, whatever may be his race, color or beliefs. They rise above every status or outlawry. They survive any popular passion or frenzy of the moment.

"While people in other lands may not share our beliefs as to due process and the dignity of the individual, we are not free to give effect to our emotions in reckless disregard for the rights of others. We live under a Constitution which is the embodiment of all the high hopes and aspirations of the new world."

In Olmstead v. U.S. (1928) the court upheld wiretapping, but Justices Oliver Wendell Holmes and Louis Brandeis dissented. Holmes declared it would be better for "some criminals to escape than that the government should play an ignoble part."

Brandeis in his dissent declared, "The makers of our Constitution undertook to secure conditions favorable to the pursuit of happiness. They conferred, as against the government, the right to be let alone--the most comprehensive of rights and the right most valued by civilized men.

"Our government is the potent, the omnipresent teacher. It teaches the whole people by its example. If the government becomes a lawbreaker it breeds contempt for the law."

After his horrible ruling in Schenck v. U.S., Holmes came to his senses with a marvelous dissent six months later in Abrams v. U.S. (1919). He deplored the 20-year prison sentence for publishing two harmless leaflets. He pointed out that the defendants were punished "not for what the indictment alleges but for the creed that they avow."

Holmes concluded with a ringing declaration of free speech: "We should be eternally vigilant against any attempts to check the expression of opinions that we loathe."

Justice Harlan F. Stone was the sole dissenter in Minersville School District v. Gobitis (1940) when the court upheld a school flag-salute statute. The Jehovah's Witnesses objected because to them saluting the flag was worshiping a graven image.

"It is a long step and one which I am unable to take to the position that government may, as a supposed educational measure, compel public affirmations which violate religious conscience," Stone wrote. "The very essence of liberty is the freedom of the individual from compulsion as to what he shall think and what he shall say. This seems to me no more than the surrender of the constitutional protection of the liberty of small minorities to the popular will."

Stone was proved right just three years later in West Virginia State Board of Education v. Barnette when Justice Robert H. Jackson made his magnificent statement about the Bill of Rights:

"The very purpose of a Bill of Rights was to withdraw certain subjects from the vicissitudes of political controversy, to place them beyond the reach of majorities and officials and to establish them as legal principles to be applied by the courts. One's right to life, liberty and property, to free speech, a free press, freedom of worship and assembly may not be submitted to a vote."

In Zorach v. Clauson (1952) the court upheld a New York public school board policy of allowing students released time to attend religious classes. Justice William O. Douglas, to his shame, wrote the majority opinion:

"We are a religious people whose institutions presuppose a Supreme Being."

In a sizzling dissent, Justice Jackson answered Douglas:

- "The day that this country ceases to be free for irreligion it will cease to be free for religion."

- "The wall which the court was professing to erect between church and state has become warped and twisted."

It is dissents like these that reflect the deeply ingrained conscience of Americans who demand freedom, equality and justice for all.

Reno News & Review, May 16, 2013

Supreme Court

Roberts kills Voting Rights Act

*After practicing law for 40 years I've observed
that when judges want to get a certain result they
have no more honesty than a used-car salesman.*

Richard Covert, letter to San Francisco Chronicle

Supreme Court Chief Justice Roberts is a master of
Jesuitical opinions: deceptive, misleading, subtle, sly,
crafty--and specious.

Roberts is also skillful at persuading liberal justices to
join his opinions. But don't you be fooled: he is a right-
wing partisan.

The result is an ever more reactionary court masked
by Robert's seeming reasonableness. His opinions are
often wrong but few people see it. The former Justice
David Souter did. He loathed Roberts for his "disrespect
of precedent, his grasping conservatism and his aggressive
pursuit of political objectives."

Nevertheless, Roberts rules the court if he can get
swingman Justice Kennedy to join his three other exponents
of reaction: Justices Scalia, Thomas and Alito.

In the 2012-2013 term just concluded the court
continued to be good for business. It showered the Chamber
of Commerce with victories:

• Cutting back on class actions suits that are essential
for fairness to "the little guy"; making it harder to sue
the makers of dangerous drugs; favoring employers
in workplace discrimination; limiting suits against
corporations for human rights abuses abroad; and allowing
companies to avoid class-actions suits through arbitration
agreements.

A perfect example of Roberts' workmanship: his

opinion stabbing the heart of the historic Voting Rights Act of 1965.

Judiciary theorist Richard Posner is merciless. He calls it: "a lame piece of work," offering weak support and a "newly invented 'fundamental principle of equal sovereignty.' " Posner concludes: "It simply does not wash."

"Voting discrimination still exists," Roberts wrote. "No one doubts that. The question is whether the act's extraordinary measures, including the disparate treatment of the states, continue to satisfy constitutional requirements."

They do not, the retrograde court ruled, 5-4. Eight states in the South are free to change election laws without U.S. approval. They are free to keep blacks from the polls with voter ID, raise barriers to early voting and to carve out discriminatory voting districts.

Roberts, living in the court's dream world, says the VRA law is "based on 40-year-old facts having no relationship to the present day." Justice Scalia is also living in that fantasy world, calling the law during oral argument a "perpetuation of racial entitlement." In other words, giving blacks something they don't deserve.

The Roberts decision was "intellectually dishonest and disingenuous," as the New York Times pointed out.

Justice Ginsburg cried out in an angry dissent joined by Justices Breyer, Kagan and Sotomayor: "Hubris is a fit word for today's demolition of VRA. The sad irony of the decision lies in its utter failure to grasp why the VRA has proven effective. The court errs egregiously.

"Early attempts to cope with this vile infection resembled battling the Hydra. Whenever one form of voting discrimination was prohibited, others sprang up in its place.

"When confronting the most constitutionally invidious form of discrimination and the most fundamental right in our democratic system, Congress's power to act is at its height.

"The Constitution vests broad powers in Congress to protect the right to vote and in particular to combat racial discrimination in voting. This court has repeatedly reaffirmed Congress' prerogative to use any rational means in exercise of its power in this area."

The Ginsburg decision was long but necessary to express her anguish. She cited the Fifteenth Amendment ratified in 1870: "The right of citizens of the United States to vote shall not be denied or abridged by the United States or any state on account of race, color or previous condition of servitude."

Ginsburg was absolutely right. But ideology reigns in the Roberts court, not reason.

Roberts and his fellow politicians, Scalia, Thomas, Alito and Kennedy, make the law.

Judges are supposed to be impartial. But whatever wrong ruling they hand down they always muster arguments for it. Roberts is very good at it--to the detriment of the nation.

This columnist refers to the Supremes as the Roberts court. But perhaps Dennis Myers, news editor of the Reno News & Review, is more perceptive. He refers to them as the Kennedy court.

In any case, Greg Palast of Truthout was so incensed by the VRA ruling that he called it the "Ku Klux Kourt," figuratively dancing on the grave of Martin Luther King. As cartoonist Garry Trudeau in Doonesbury puts it: "the return of Jimmy Crow" allows voter suppression.

It's a subtle form of apartheid 148 years after the Civil War ended.

Sparks Tribune, July 11, 2013

Court decries gay couple hatred

The Supreme Court leaped into the 21st century recently by nullifying the 1996 Defense of Marriage Act (DOMA), catching up with public opinion favoring gay marriage.

The court, with the usual 5-4 "political" split, ruled that married same-sex couples are entitled to federal benefits such as health care, Social Security, life insurance and survivor tax policies.

Edith Windsor of New York offers a good example of how survivors in gay marriages will benefit. When her female partner died the IRS refused to treat her as a surviving spouse as it would have for a husband. She was assessed a tax bill of $363,000 for inheritance of her partner's estate.

Justice Kennedy, writing the majority opinion, declared: "DOMA instructed all people with whom same-sex couples interact, including their own children, that their marriage is less worthy than the marriage of others." He said the statute disparaged the dignity of gay couples.

Adam Liptak, Supreme Court reporter for the New York Times, noted that Kennedy announced the opinion to a hushed courtroom "in a stately tone that indicated he was delivering a civil rights landmark."

He was. Justices Breyer, Ginsburg, Kagan and Sotomayor joined his opinion.

Antediluvian sourpuss Justice Scalia complained in his bitter dissent that "anyone opposed to same-sex marriage is an enemy of human decency." He slammed the Kennedy opinion as "a jaw-dropping assertion of judicial supremacy over the will of the people expressed by Congress."

But the determination of the people is often wrong as it was in California's vote to ban gay marriage in Proposition 8.

Other DOMA dissenters were Chief Justice Roberts

and Justices Thomas and Alito. Roberts, during oral argument, argued that the institution of marriage "didn't include homosexual couples." He was wrong.

The reality is that gay characters and celebrities are prevalent in America: TV, sports and rap music. Thirty percent of the population lives in states that allow same-sex marriage.

As Martin Luther King said: "The arc of the moral universe is long but it bends toward justice." It did just that in the DOMA ruling.

Affirmative action defeat

The court punted on affirmative action, sending a case originating at the University of Texas, Austin, back to the lower courts for stricter scrutiny.

That means the court, by a 7-1 vote, no longer deems affirmative action necessary. Justice Scalia expressed that view by saying he would overturn any racial preferences.

But Justice Ginsburg in dissent set him and the court straight. She said the plan to take students from the top 10 percent of the state's public high schools was adopted to combat racially segregated schools and neighborhoods.

Ginsburg, a former civil rights lawyer, declared:

"Only an ostrich could regard the supposedly neutral alternatives as race unconscious. State universities need not be blind to the lingering effects of an overtly discriminatory past, the legacy of law-sanctioned inequality.

"Race-consciousness is preferable to some backdoor effort to address inequality by concealing mention of it. Moreover, the University of Texas considers race as but one of many factors in the admissions process."

Justice Ginsburg is so tiny that at oral arguments before the Supreme Court she is barely visible behind the high bench. But her heart and mind are mighty. Amid the dismal Roberts Court, she is stellar.

Surveillance ruling wrong

The Supreme Court almost always rules for the government in national security cases. So it was hardly a surprise that the court recently rejected a challenge to the broadened power of government to eavesdrop on international phone calls and emails.

Writing for the Backward Five in the 5-4 vote, Justice Alito said journalists, lawyers and human rights advocates were unable to show how the congressional law harmed them. He dusted off the ancient court standby: they lacked standing to sue.

Alito, in a circuitous argument, said only the government knows whether the plaintiffs' communications have been intercepted. So he said it was the plaintiffs' burden to prove that they have standing "by pointing to specific facts, not the government's burden to disprove standing by revealing details of its surveillance priorities."

Justice Breyer dissented, joined by the other rational justices, Ginsburg, Kagan and Sotomayor. Breyer declared that the harm done to the plaintiffs was not speculative.

"Indeed, it is as likely to take place as are most future events that common sense inference and ordinary knowledge of human nature tell us will happen," he added.

True. But, alas, the prevailing Supremes are so partisan that common sense means nothing to them.

Sparks Tribune, July 18, 2013

Supremes ignorant of gay marriage

The Supreme Court justices are wandering in the Dark Ages on gay marriage, cloistered in their ivory tower, isolated from real people in the real world.

During recent oral arguments the justices showed gross ignorance of the subject, its history and the long struggle for gay and lesbian equality.

Justice Alito complained that "same-sex marriage was very new." He apparently never heard of the Stonewall riots, a series of demonstrations in 1969 by gays against a police raid at the Stonewall Inn in New York City's Greenwich Village.

It was the beginning of the gay liberation movement like the beginning of women's liberation at Seneca Falls, N.Y., in 1848 and the beginning of black liberation at Selma, Ala., in 1965.

Many justices seemed unaware that the term gay has long been used instead of homosexual. Some spoke of the "sanctity of marriage," oblivious of the fact that 50 percent of marriages end in divorce.

The saddest aspect of the oral arguments was the right-wing views of two usual liberals, Justices Ginsburg and Sotomayor. Their queasiness was dumbfounding.

"We let issues perk and so we let racial segregation perk for 56 years from 1898 to 1954," Sotomayor said. Perk? An absurdity. Fifty-six years is much too long to end injustice. Sotomayor uttered more nonsense about the states and society needing more time "to figure out" its stance on gay marriage.

She too was sleeping like Rip Van Winkle through the whole same-sex marriage controversy. Ginsburg, while approving the Roe decision, has lectured constantly that the abortion issue "moved too far, too fast." More nonsense from a justice who should know better.

189

While the reactionary Scalia railed about the "possible destructive effects" of gay couples adopting children, Justice Kennedy rightly observed that "40,000 children in California living with gay parents want their parents to have full recognition and status."

Yet Kennedy wrongly argued for the right of states to regulate marriage. Gay marriage is a constitutional matter, not something that should be made law by political cretins in state legislatures and by retrograde state voters.

California voters decided in Proposition 8 to ban gay marriage. It was a perfect example of the public being wrong. Columnist Maureen Dowd of the New York Times zeroed in on the problem: "civil rights should not hinge on the whims of the people."

And The Nation columnist Melissa Harris-Perry pointed to another truth: "For decades LGBT (gay, lesbian, bisexual and transgender) people have had families built on commitment, love and parental devotion. Moreover, marriage equality will extend a basic civil right and allow LGBT Americans to get the economic protections associated with matrimony."

They deserve all those rights.

Take the case of Edie Windsor of New York. When her female married partner died the law did not allow the IRS to treat her as a surviving spouse as it would have for a husband. She was assessed a tax bill of $363,000 for inheritance of her partner's estate.

As for the Defense of Marriage Act (DOMA), it is indefensible. Justice Kagan noted the act was passed by Congress out of "dislike, animus and fear."

Whatever the court rules in June, the battle is already won. Respondents to a nationwide poll recently said they approved of gay marriage 58 to 36 percent. The margin was wider among young people: 81 percent. Even right-wing kook Rush Limbaugh admitted "the issue is lost."

190

Roberts indulged in legalisms that skirted the issue. He questioned whether the people challenging Proposition 8 had standing (the right to sue). He expressed irritation that the issue was before the court. He argued fatuously that the institution of marriage "didn't include homosexual couples."

President Clinton, the gutless wonder, shamefully signed the DOMA under the cover of darkness in 1996. He admitted recently his regret at signing the bill. The truth is he feared backlash in an election year.

The law was wrong then as it is now. But as they often do, presidents act for political reasons rather than humanity.

In Loving v. Virginia in 1967 the Warren Court ruled that interracial marriage was "essential to the pursuit of happiness." The decision paved the way for Justice Thomas, an African-American, to marry his white wife.

There never is a "right time" to end discrimination. The time is now, not the delay the Supreme Court promises. As Martin Luther King said: "The arc of the moral universe is long but it bends toward justice."

Ames (Iowa) Tribune, April 18, 2013

191

Justices blind on cameras

Members of government institutions sooner or later take on the coloration of that institution.

Take the cases of Justices Sotomayor and Kagan. Both were in favor of camera coverage of Supreme Court oral arguments.

During her confirmation hearings in 2009 Sotomayor was ardently in favor of letting citizens see the Supreme Court at work.

"I have had positive experiences with cameras," she said about serving on U.S. district and circuit courts. "I have happily joined experiments using cameras in my courtroom."

But after four years on the Supreme Court she changed her mind. She now opposes cameras in court. She has become an "upper class snob" just like the other justices who adamantly oppose cameras.

She argues fallaciously that most Americans would not understand Supreme Court arguments and there was no point "in letting them try." Most Americans couldn't care less about the Supreme Court. But for many who do care camera coverage is important.

Adam Liptak, New York Times Supreme Court reporter, labels the Sotomayor comment "an intellectual poll tax that could just as well limit attendance in the courtroom."

Justice Kagan has also done a volte-face. At her confirmation hearings in 2010 she said courtroom cameras "would be a great thing for the institution and, more important, a great thing for the American people."

Now she claims "people might play to the camera" and coverage could be misused. Ridiculous. My experience attending a Supreme Court oral argument revealed extreme respect and even deference to the justices.

The Canadian Supreme Court has televised oral arguments for two decades. Recently that court streamed live on the Internet. Owen Rees, the court's executive director, says "filming has increased the public's access to the court and understanding of its work."

True. But the U.S. Supreme Court insists it is "different." Nonsense. It is unable to give convincing reasons for still veiling the court in the 21st century.

As Kyu Youin, journalism professor and First Amendment scholar at the University of Oregon, remarks: the U.S. Supreme Court betrays "a distinctly American commitment to free expression."

"Many people outside the U.S. are wondering why it is so calcified in its thinking about cameras in the Supreme Court," Youin added.

Answer: because it is also calcified about many of the decisions it hands down.

No consumer recourse

In one of its calcified rulings recently, the court held that consumers seriously harmed by generic drugs don't deserve compensation.

The court, by the usual Retrograde Five margin of 5-4, overturned a lower court decision that awarded $21 million to a woman for pain and suffering caused by reaction to a generic drug. The ruling, which leaves people harmed by generic drugs no recourse, accounts for more than 80 percent of all prescriptions.

As the New York Times editorialized: "It is imperative that the Food and Drug Administration write protective regulations holding generic companies liable for any harm their products cause."

The Times paints a grim picture. The woman, Karen Bartlett of New Hampshire, suffered dreadful injuries after taking a generic version of an anti-inflammatory drug, sulindac, for shoulder pain.

"She developed an extremely severe reaction in which two-thirds of her skin sloughed off," the Times said. "She was left permanently disfigured, legally blind and with permanent damage to her lungs and esophagus."

Justice Alioto, writing for the majority, said the generic company, Mutual Pharmaceutical, was not liable because it had no power to unilaterally change the chemicals or the warning label.

It's a typical made-up reason for a court decision. As the liberal dissenters declared, the company should pay compensation for any harm done and consider taking the drug off the market.

Bar to deportation

In a victory for fairness, the Supreme Court recently ruled, 7-2, that a conviction for marijuana distribution under Georgia law should not result in automatic deportation. A Jamaican, legally in the United States, was ordered deported by an immigration judge.

His offense? Possessing 1.3 grams of pot. The amount makes two cigarettes.

Justice Sotomayor, writing for the majority, noted the absurdity of deportation for a mere misdemeanor.

Wise DNA ruling

The 2012-2013 term just ended produced a wise decision: a ruling that genes are not patentable. It declared unanimously that human DNA isolated from a chromosome cannot be patented because it is a product of nature.

Justice Thomas, in his opinion for the court, declared that granting patents on natural phenomena would inhibit innovation, "at odds with the very point of patents: promotion of creation."

Sparks Tribune, July 25, 2013

194

Inside Supreme Court

THE OATH
The Obama White House and the Supreme Court
By Jeffrey Toobin
Doubleday, 298 pages, 2012

This is an important inside look at the Supreme Court but a badly titled book.

The botched oath of office administered by Chief Justice John Roberts to president-elect Barack Obama in 2009 has nothing to do with their sharp disagreement about constitutional interpretation.

Yet author Jeffrey Toobin opens the book with the trivial mistake and goes on and on about a matter of no consequence.

Obama, a constitutional law professor with liberal instincts, was bound to clash with a reactionary chief justice.

In that quarrel, President Obama is right, Roberts wrong. As Toobin puts it: Roberts "has far more often used his formidable skills on behalf of the strong in opposition to the weak." Toobin also rightly said: "The Obama team regards the Supreme Court as just another group of Republicans."

But the chief justice is enormously powerful as shown by his court's retrograde Citizens United ruling of 2010. That decision allowed unlimited campaign funding by declaring money speech protected by the First Amendment.

As wrong as the Roberts decision was, it remains the law of the land. The odds on a constitutional amendment to reverse it are prohibitive.

Toobin is wonderful on Justice Ginzburg, a tiny woman with a huge heart. She disagreed with Justice Blackmun that abortion is a privacy matter.

"Abortion rights are about equality," she said. "The denial of abortion rights to women is just another former of discrimination."

Toobin notes that Ginzburg particularly resented the patronizing of Justice Kennedy in his Carhart abortion decision of 2007, a ruling "straight out of the anti-abortion movement in which he refers to the fetus as a 'baby' and a 'child.' "

It is such "inside stuff" that enhances the Toobin book. Such as: "Liberals want flexible rules that allow courts to reach decisions on the merits and conservatives want strict rules to prevent cases from being heard."

Such as: the court's surprising rule for Obamacare: "Roberts deferred as justices have for 75 years to Congress on issues relating to managing the economy. But it was folly to pretend that Roberts had discovered his inner moderate."

Such as: justices so often try to achieve political results rather than adjudicate cases.

Such as: moderate Republican ideas, like moderate Republicans, have disappeared from the court as they have from the nation.

Such as: Latina Justice Sotomayor proudly declaring: "I am a product of affirmative action."

Such as: Justices Scalia and Breyer are show-offs and Justice Alito writes "clunky sentences" while Justice Breyer opinions ramble.

Toobin sparkles on Justice Souter who declared that the Bush v. Gore decision of 2000 giving the presidency to G.W. Bush "was so political, so transparent that it scarred Souter's belief in the Supreme Court as an institution."

Yet Scalia, confronted by hostile audiences on his frequent speaking tours, could say nothing more intelligent than: "Oh get over it." (That's someone who Toobin describes as an intellectual.)

Souter "came to loathe the Roberts Court," denouncing "its disrespect for precedent, its grasping conservatism and its aggressive pursuit of political objectives."

Toobin is excellent too on Scalia, ridiculing his notions about textualism and originalism, the idea that rights do not exist if they are not stated in the Constitution. Scalia's absurd views ignore the wisdom of Justice Holmes: the law responds to "the felt necessities of the time."

Toobin notes Scalia's hunger to have been named chief justice. He cites Scalia's "belligerence at oral arguments as a way of getting attention--his craving for the spotlight." And declares that Scalia is a conservative "who became a right-wing crank."

That aside, the book is too long by about 100 pages as many books published today are. It's too wordy, desperately needing a stern editor. But Toobin is a star Supreme Court reporter for the New Yorker. Magazine and book editors rarely edit "stars."

Toobin writes about standing--the right to be heard by the Supreme Court--an arcane matter of interest only to lawyers. He writes too much about Justice O'Connor, who had long since left the court. His book is full of clichés, is repetitive and overuses useless "of courses."

Nevertheless, Toobin makes it clear that the Roberts Court is a partisan bunch of Republicans lawmakers harming the nation.

Sparks Tribune, Jan. 10, 2013

History

French invasion revives colonialism

What's past is prologue.

Shakespeare's "The Tempest"

France's recent military intervention in Mali is hard to believe coming from its socialist president, François Hollande.

Hollande, who campaigned as an anti-war candidate, sent fighter jets and troops into the former French colony in west Africa. It was not just a revival of colonialism. It meant he has learned nothing from the history of France's futile colonial wars in Vietnam and Algeria.

He's acting like any American president in intervening where the country does not belong.

Hollande assured the French people that the fighting force would leave Mali quickly. But it is a familiar story we have heard from U.S. presidents.

The United States is training and funding local militaries and giving logistical and intelligence support to African Union forces. President Obama said U.S. support would be limited. That's also a story the American people have heard before.

Both countries have intervened on behalf of the government in northern Mali in order to thwart the rebels fighting under the banner of Islam and al-Qaida.

It's a desert version of the follies of Vietnam and Afghanistan. But the French and Americans never learn from history.

Women in combat

The moth-ridden Pentagon has surprisingly ended its ban on women in combat. However belated, the decision was what the New York Times called "a triumph for common sense."

201

Its editorial added: "By opening infantry, artillery and other battlefield jobs to all qualified service members regardless of sex, the military is showing that discrimination has no place in a society that proclaims opportunity.

"Women have been in the thick of combat in Iraq and Afghanistan for more than a decade. More than 280,000 have been deployed there. Thousands have been injured and 150 killed."

Opponents to ending the ban have argued that women captured in battle would be raped. But the Pentagon knows that military women face a far greater danger of sexual assault and harassment from fellow soldiers.

$500 million pals

Amgen, the pharmaceutical giant, got a two-year reprieve from paying up to $500 million over a two-year period to the Medicare program because of congressional buddies.

The huge loophole in a financial package was passed on New Year's Eve when no one was looking. It was created by Amgen's Senate cronies: Republicans Mitch McConnell and Orrin Hatch and Democrat Max Baucus.

"A trio of perpetrators who treat the U.S. Treasury as if it were a cash-and-carry annex of corporate America," Bill Moyers rightly characterized it.

But as everyone who follows politics knows, Congress does the bidding of the big contributors to political campaigns. It helps, too, to have the enormous financial resources of Amgen. The firm has 74 lobbyists in Washington. (Amgen, the world's largest biotechnology company, specializes in kidney dialysis and a pill called Sensipar.)

The influence of the powerful prevailed despite the fact that Amgen recently pleaded guilty to marketing an antianemia drug illegally. It was assessed civil and criminal penalties of $762 million.

It is such corporate welfare that adds to the ever-growing cost of health care for the American people.

Pitiful minimum wage

The federal minimum wage has been stuck on $7.25 an hour since 2009. It is not tied to inflation, which means $290 for a 40-hour week doesn't go far.

Ten states, which do tie their minimum wage to inflation rates, offer a pay rate higher than the federal minimum. The state of Washington is highest, requiring a minimum wage of $9.19.

Congress takes care of the rich. The vast majority of Americans get little help from federal lawmakers.

More colonialism

The Argentine writer Jorge Luis Borges described the squabbling over the Falklands as two bald men fighting over a comb.

He's right. The inhospitable, craggy archipelago 310 miles from Argentina in the South Atlantic has fewer than 3,000 inhabitants.

Nevertheless, Argentine rightly claims the islands (Malvinas). The British, however, possess the Falklands so the age of colonialism lingers.

Sparks Tribune, Jan. 31, 2013

Brits keep anachronistic colonies

Nations are pieces on a chessboard on which is being played out a great game for the domination of the world.

Lord Curzon, viceroy of India, in 1898

Colonialism no longer dominates the world but its evil still exists.

The British seized Gibraltar in 1704. Four centuries later the Brits are still squatting on Spanish land, a 2.5 miles long and three-quarter mile wide isthmus jutting into the Mediterranean.

The UN General Assembly approved decolonization of the "Rock" in 1963. Yet the 28,000 British in Gibraltar voted to remain part of the British Empire.

Spineless Britain cannot say nay to a "vote of the people" so it perpetuates a colonial anachronism. It is the only such territory in Europe. The same situation exists for the Malvinas (Falklands), an archipelago of two large islands and 776 smaller ones on Argentina soil in the Strait of Magellan.

At various times the island chain has had French, British, Spanish and Argentine settlements. But Britain declared ownership in 1833. A dispute flared in the 1950s when Argentine ruler Juan Peron asserted Argentine sovereignty. The Brits were unmoved.

Then in the 1960s tension arose again when the UN passed a resolution on decolonization. But negotiations never got anywhere because the Brits insisted they were the rightful owners. It took that position because the Falkland Islanders--all 3,000 of them!--voted to remain English.

Falkland residents prevailed over justice.

Prime Minister Margaret Thatcher of Great Britain guaranteed the seizure with a mini-war in 1982. This latter-day colonialism was so macho the warmongering Brits re-elected a reactionary ruler.

The UK Guardian, liberal-leftist newspaper, dared to call the islands by their real name: Malvinas. For that truth-telling it was denounced in Britain for "defying national pride."

'Pocket stuffer' loses

We have a do-nothing Congress but occasionally some of its committees do something wonderful like opposing Larry Summers in his bid to become chairman of the Federal Reserve Board.

The result: he withdrew after the Senate Banking Committee made it plain that it held too many no votes.

Senator Elizabeth Warren of Massachusetts was among the key committee members leading the opposition. She is one of the precious few genuine liberals in the Senate, worthy of being the first woman president of the United States. (Which is why she never will be president.)

The Summers withdrawal opens the way for the excellent Janet Yellen, Fed vice-chair, to succeed Ben Bernanke.

Summers was one of President Obama's economic advisers, serving government but preferring "to stuff his pockets" in the private sector. As columnist Maureen Dowd put it: "He is an exemplar of the obscenely lucrative revolving-door problem, part of the culture that ran the economy into the ground."

That culture espoused Wall Street deregulation, bailouts for bankers who were "too big to fail" and outsourcing.

Summers, speaking to world business leaders in 2011, said they should not oppose offshoring. He likened critics to "Luddites who took axes to machinery early in England's industrial revolution."

U.S. firms are able to sell products cheaply because they are produced overseas. Workers there make something like

35 cents an hour and are terribly overworked. No wonder their out-sourced products are shoddy.

I bought a pair of slippers made in China. In several weeks the seams began to unravel. Soon they disintegrated into a worthless mess. I bought some belts made in Thailand. They gleamed but were stiff, containing more cardboard than leather.

Better to pay more for merchandise than buy shabby goods.

'Miracle plant' approved

California, legalizing growth of the "miracle plant," is expected to reap $500 million annually from its newest industry.

Gov. Jerry Brown, overcoming puritanical objections, signed a bill vetoed by three previous California governors to legalize industrial hemp. California copies nine other states and 30 countries, among them Canada, France, Germany, Great Britain and China.

State Senator Mark Leno of San Francisco, who has championed such a measure since 2005, was ecstatic.

"It's renewable every 90 days, grows without herbicides, pesticides and fungicides, and needs less water than corn does," Leno notes. "It's the definition of sustainability."

U.S. Attorney General Eric Holder apparently wiped away previous federal objections to hemp-growing. Holder said that if a state passes a law allowing and regulating marijuana the government would not intervene.

Hemp, a "cousin" of marijuana (cannabis sativa), has been cultivated throughout history for fiber, seed, food, medicine--and even religious and spiritual uplift. It is also refined to make wax, resin, fuel and cloth.

Government officials sometimes do the right thing.

Sparks Tribune, Oct. 24, 2013

Capitalism has no soul

Books spur march to socialism

*For justice thunders condemnation...a better
world's in place. The international party shall be
the human race.*

L'Internationale," leftist fight song

*Socialism has inspired almost every gain in
human freedom in modern times.*

Michael Harrington,
"Socialism Past and Future"

The poet Alexander Pope advised that "a little learning"
is a dangerous thing so we should "drink deep or taste
not the Pierian spring" (mythological Macedonian site of
knowledge).

I determined as a young man to "drink deep," to rout
my ignorance. So I read works on a list of "the most
important 100 books." Included were the great "Ulysses"
by Joyce, an ode to human survival in "One Day in the
Life of Ivan Denisovich" by Solzhenitsyn, the classic
"Walden" by Thoreau and stories of "unimportant" people
in "Working" by Studs Terkel.

It was the beginning of a long march to socialism.

After graduating from Penn State in 1953, I spent two
years in the army. One guy in my barracks said of me:
"That cat's always reading!"

Indeed I was. "Red Badge of Courage" by Crane,
"Candide" by Voltaire, "Sons and Lovers" by D.H.
Lawrence and "Devils of Loudon" and "Antic Hay" by
Aldous Huxley. And many, many more.

I voted for the first time in 1956, choosing the Democrat

Stevenson over Republican Eisenhower. I long ago had liberal genes. Then I read such books as:

Steinbeck's "The Grapes of Wrath" portraying the injustices suffered by migrant workers. Its vividness turns any sensitive reader to socialism. Likewise with "Germinal" by Zola showing French coal miners suffering the exploitation of capitalism and Hugo's "Les Misérables," portraying the gross injustices of life.

Harrington's "The Other America" depicts poverty in this land of plenty. The reform-minded Dickens cried out against child labor in "David Copperfield." Orwell revealed poverty in "Down and Out in Paris and London." "The Wretched of the Earth" by Frantz Fanon is a savage indictment of colonialism.

"Native Son" and "Black Boy" by Richard Wright and "The Autobiography of Malcolm X" portray the horror of being black in apartheid America. "The Second Sex" by Simone de Beauvoir, an educational feminist book before the word was commonly used. Joseph Heller's "Catch-22" shows the stupidity and butchery of war.

Reading inculcated in me a deep feeling for the downtrodden, the outcast, the despised, the put-upon and the victims of discrimination. Adelle Davis, food faddist, said you are what you eat. No, we are what we read, as journalism teacher Deidre Pike once noted in a RN&R column.

Socialism means social justice. It means equality. It means brotherhood, what the Germans call *bruderschaft.* It means cooperation rather than competition. It means that the qualities of economic life are central to the quality of life. L'Humanité, French Communist Party newspaper, is well named: humanity.

Capitalism is crass. It considers making money the most important thing in life. It stresses profits rather than human needs. It is an unholy pursuit of "filthy lucre." It is obscene.

Capitalism is selfish. It means plutocracy. One percenters rule. It is unfettered and unregulated. It means outsourcing and union-breaking. Capitalism can never have a human face. In stark contrast, Russia's Gorbachev showed us communism with a human face.

Cato the Elder of ancient Rome decried Carthage, declaring it must be destroyed. If America is ever to have true egalitarianism it must destroy capitalism.

Plato was the first writer to mention utopia. In "The Republic" (4th century B.C.) he wrote of the perfect city requiring either that "kings be philosophers or philosophers be kings." He urged justice in a just state.

"Utopia" by Thomas More (1516) revealed a passionate concern for the human condition. He was dedicated to the improvement of society. More declared that the function of government was to serve the people. (Surely the most utopian concept in all history!)

"A map of the world that does not include Utopia is not worth even glancing at," Oscar Wilde wrote in "The Soul of Man Under Socialism."

"The Communist Manifesto" (1848) by Karl Marx and Friedrich Engels is the socialist bible, the most famous and influential pamphlet ever written. It sums up the Marx oeuvre, history's most savage criticism of capitalism. Marx remains the world's greatest economist, dwarfing the puny conservative economists in American business schools today.

Engels in a preface to the 1888 English edition of the Manifesto wrote: "It is undoubtedly the most widespread, the most international production of all socialist literature, the common platform acknowledged by millions of workingmen from Siberia to California."

The first section of the Manifesto opens with: "The history of all hitherto existing society is the history of class struggle." Still true in America today. Another truth in America today is in the Manifesto: "jurisprudence is but the will of your class (bourgeois) made the law for all." Section three of the Manifesto speaks of "the crying inequalities in the distribution of wealth." Still true in America.

Eugene McCarraher, Villanova professor, wrote a marvelous précis of the Marx thesis in a Nation article:

• Capitalism is pernicious and incorrigibly avaricious.

• Capitalism is "a giant vortex of accumulation."

• Capitalism is unjust, amoral and rapacious.

• "Capitalism compels us to be greedy, callous and petty."

• "The rage to accumulate remains the predatory heart and soul of capitalism."

Thoreau complained 150 years ago that all Americans do is "work, work, work." Columnist Robert Reich comes to the same conclusion today. He offers what he calls "a bold proposal": three weeks of paid vacation every year for every worker.

"Most Americans get only two weeks vacation," Reich writes. "One in four gets no paid vacation, not even holidays."

True. But to civilized nations there's nothing bold about his proposal.

France has six-week vacations. The European Union requires a four-week vacation. Europe has more paid holidays than America does. France has long mandated a 35-hour week.

That's socialism--hardly to be despised in socially backward America.

Roughly 40 million U.S. workers in the private sector don't get paid for sick days. The federal minimum wage is a paltry $7.25 an hour. It was passed by Congress in 2007 but since ravaged by inflation. Millions of Americans make less than $7.25 an hour. Many workers fall below the poverty line.

A new book by Christopher Hayes, "Twilight of the Elites," provides a damning insight: "The 1 percent and the nation's governing class are the same."

America boasts of its one person-one vote democracy but government favors the One Percent. The system begins with presidential advisers.

"To replace the multimillionaire Rahm Emanuel, the multimillionaire President Obama (net worth $5 million) named multimillionaire William Daley. Daley was replaced by Jack Lew, who spent four years with Citigroup where he got a bonus of $950,000 in 2009."

Obama's economic advisers pass through a revolving door from the private sector to the public service, rich white men getting huge consulting fees and flying in private jets.

Power attorneys make $10 million a year manipulating the loophole-ridden tax code to enable plutocrats to keep scores of billions from the IRS. In 2007 the richest 400 taxpayers had more money then 150 million Americans put together. America's 10 most profitable corporations paid an average tax of 9 percent in 2011. ExxonMobil got away with paying 2 percent.

Mitt Romney, GOP presidential nominee, paid just 13 percent for decades on an annual income of $20 million. Even Adam Smith, apostle of the free market and exponent of the "hidden hand" that supposedly benefits everyone in society, advocated a graduated income tax.

Nearly one-half of the 535 members of Congress are millionaires. The Bush tax cuts handed $82 billion to the One Percenters. Obama, a gutless wonder, extended them.

The "cult of smartness" is an obsession of the elites, author Hayes points out. Justice Scalia of the Supreme

Court is more "intelligent" than Justices Sotomayor and Kagan. Yet his judicial views are narrow and inhumane. Sotomayor and Kagan are worth more than one hundred Scalias.

The 99 percent believe that government does not and will not work for them. They are right.

The Manifesto urges us to "rescue education from the influence of the ruling class." Because of that ruling class many Americans derive U.S. exceptionalism from their high school history. The notion is absurd if you read Howard Zinn's "A People's History of the United States" or James Loewen's "Lies My Teacher Told Me."

America so often supports worldwide dictators because they are on "our side." It does not practice what it preaches. It overthrows "disobedient" worldwide governments.

In 1953 Britain and America overthrew Iranian prime minister Mossadegh because he dared nationalize the Anglo-Iranian oil company. In his place the unholy alliance reinstated the Shah, who had been ousted in the Iranian revolution. During the 1980s America armed the rebels in Nicaragua to defeat the leftist Sandinistas. America destabilized the economy and supported death squads.

Americans revile communist Cuba. Yet those "godless commies" have universal health care, free college education, free day care and 12-week paid maternity leave. That's humane socialism.

America's heartless capitalism has none of those civilized measures. Yet the United States has invaded and tried to overthrow the Cuban government because it is alien to the capitalist credo.

The democratically elected Allende embarked on a socialist agenda to lift the living standards of Chileans. But an angry President Nixon launched an economic blockade. The most cynical of the Nixon gang, Secretary of State Henry Kissinger, told the CIA station chief in Santiago that U.S. policy demands that "Allende be overthrown in a coup." He was.

Kissinger arrogantly declared that America had to act because "the Chilean people did not know what was good for them." (Allende was murdered in the 1973 coup.) No wonder comedian Tom Lehrer cracked: "Satire died the day they gave the Nobel Peace Prize to Kissinger."

9/11 caused much "weeping and gnashing of teeth." But it was tiny retribution for 150 years of unjustified U.S. invasions, killings and coups. It was deserved payback for the U.S. military presence in the Middle East and its purblind support of Israel.

Wilde wrote in "The Soul of Man Under Socialism": "The most tragic fact in the French Revolution is not that Marie Antoinette was killed for being a queen but that starved peasants of the Vendée died for the hideous cause of feudalism."

Still today many Americans vote against their own economic interests as Thomas Frank notes in his book, "What's the Matter with Kansas?" An example of such blinders occurred in the recall election of Wisconsin's Republican Governor Walker earlier this year. Thirty-eight percent of union workers voted to retain the *union-busting governor*.

No union member should ever vote Republican. People should never vote Republican unless they are One Percenters.

In art you have two unforgettable "socialist" works.

One is the photo "Migrant Mother" (1936) taken by Dorothea Lange. The mother's face is grim, weather-beaten, worried. Two children hide their heads behind her shoulders. An infant is swaddled on her lap. Sensitive souls cannot look at that picture without becoming a socialist.

Neither can you gaze at van Gogh's "The Potato Eaters" without becoming a socialist. The gnarled faces.

The humble repast. The picture reminds you of the Edwin Markham lines in "The Man With the Hoe": "stolid and stunned, a brother to the ox."

Privatization? Canadian law mandates free airtime on radio and TV for political parties during election campaigns. In privatized America politicians pay for broadcast political advertising. The cost is enormous, amounting to $3 billion this presidential election year. Broadcasters should not profit for providing an essential service to society.

Another tragedy of history is that social revolutions get sold out: Stalin in Russia, Mao Zedong in China and Napoleon in France. (The United States, unfortunately, has never had a social revolution.) Stalin's crimes have few parallels in history: murders, purges, gulags, show trials, persecutions and assassination of dissidents like Trotsky.

But look at what the Bolshevik Revolution did do: established full citizenship for women including the right to vote, set labor laws that provided equal pay, introduced civil marriage, allowed divorce and legalized abortion.

Lincoln gave off a whiff of socialism in his message to Congress in 1861: "Labor is prior to and independent of capital. Capital is only the fruit of labor and could never have existed if labor had not first existed. Labor is the superior of capital and deserves much the higher consideration."

At the end of the 19th century the People's Party (populists) promulgated the most radical political platform that America has ever seen. At its 1892 founding convention in Omaha, Neb., these were some of its planks:

• Women's suffrage. (Women did not get the right to vote until ratification of the 19th Amendment in 1920.)

• Eight-hour day. (Then considered utopia carried to absurdity.)

• Graduated income tax. (The 16th Amendment ratified in 1913 provided for an income tax.)

• Demanded labor's right to organize 44 years before the Wagner Act did so.

Henry Demarest Lloyd declared at a populist rally in 1894: "The People's Party is more than the organized discontent of the people. It is the organized aspiration of the people for a fuller, nobler, richer, kinder life for every man, woman and child in the ranks of humanity."

The populist party, despite its mass appeal, made the fatal mistake of merging with the Democrats.

The Muckraking Age, roughly from 1902 to 1912, was the most glorious era in U.S. journalism. Some of the most famous muckrakers were Upton Sinclair, Lincoln Steffens and Ida Tarbell.

Sinclair's "The Jungle" (1906) exposed the beef trust, "the incarnation of blind and insensate greed, the spirit of capitalism made flesh." Sinclair wrote that he "aimed at the public's heart and by accident hit it in the stomach." His book led to the Pure Food and Drug Act and the Meat Inspection Act in 1906.

Tarbell wrote a series of articles in McClure's muckraking magazine blasting Standard Oil, the epitome of Gilded Age robber barons. It was turned into a book called the most important business book ever written. Steffens excoriated municipal corruption in "The Shame of the Cities."

C.C. Regier, muckraker historian, noted the effect of specific muckraking articles: "child labor was abolished, the Newlands Act of 1902 made reclamation of millions of acres of land possible (Francis Newlands was then a U.S. representative from Nevada), eight-hour laws for women were passed and workmen's compensation laws were enacted."

But the muckraking era, as wonderful as it was, did not go far enough. It was not radical by definition: going to the root of the capitalist evil.

Seymour Lipset and Gary Marks explain in "It Didn't Happen Here" (2000) the reasons socialism failed in America:

• Third-party presidential candidates are doomed by the stranglehold of the two major parties, candidates with mere pluralities win without a runoff as in French presidential elections, and the Electoral College makes it impossible for a third-party candidate to win. (The third-party campaign of Ralph Nader in 2000--to the everlasting shame of his huge ego--cost the election of a liberal president.)

• Americans lack working-class consciousness because they mistakenly think they already live in a classless society.

• Many immigrants were Catholics. As a Milwaukee archbishop said: "You can't be a Catholic and a socialist." (Theologian Paul Tillich disagreed. "Any serious Christian must be a socialist," he pointed out.)

• Socialism is associated with atheism, abhorrent to so many Americans.

• Socialists, like Unitarians in religion, attract intellectuals, college professors and university graduates--but not many voters. (Just five of us belonged to the late Reno communist cell. Three were Ph.Ds and two had master's degrees.)

Newspapers and magazines nibble around the edges of capitalism, attacking its excesses and wrong-doings but never confronting its evil. (Similarly, the Establishment press never prints articles questioning the existence of God.)

Some bankers argue that they are doing "God's work" by sustaining the free-market system. Yet Matthew 6:24 is anti-capitalist to the core: "Ye cannot serve God and mammon."

Ayn Rand became the high priestess of capitalism after her novel, "Atlas Shrugged," was published in 1957. Her philosophy was expressed in a collection of essays in 1964 entitled 'The Virtue of Selfishness."

She exemplified unfettered capitalism, wearing a brooch shaped like a dollar sign. When she died in 1982 a six-foot dollar sign stood beside her coffin.

Lenin asked in his 1902 book: "What Is To Be Done?" He answered 15 years later with the Russian Revolution. Reform is not enough. Socialism is the only answer.

Capitalism has no soul. America will be soulless until it is wise enough to adopt socialism.

Reno News & Review, Nov. 15, 2012